The Power Conundrum

The Power Conundrum

EXPLORING THE PUZZLE OF HOW TO RECLAIM A DEMOCRACY

by

Stephen Shaw

ARB Press

2021

ISBN: 978-1-7346825-0-2

Names: Shaw, Stephen (Stephen Kerr), 1954- author.
Title: The power conundrum : exploring the puzzle of how to reclaim a democracy /
Stephen Shaw.
Description: Brunswick, Maine : ARB Press, [2021]
Identifiers: ISBN 9781734682502
Subjects: LCSH: Power (Social sciences) | Democracy. | Social systems. | Self-organizing
systems. | Equality. | BISAC: POLITICAL SCIENCE / Political Ideologies / Democracy.
| POLITICAL SCIENCE / Political Process / General. | SOCIAL SCIENCE / Social
Classes & Economic Disparity.
Classification: LCC HN49.P6 S53 2021 | DDC 303.33--dc23

To my parents, David Shaw and Gretchen Van Tassel Shaw

CONTENTS

INTRODUCTION

It is a reasonable question to ask: "How can it be that humans have not managed to solve the central problems of civilization yet?" We are exceedingly clever, creative, hard-working, and caring. We have had time in abundance and no shortage of opportunities to learn from history to help in the quest for a better world.

I am left to guess that the matters of war, poverty, environmental degradation, and social injustice are not understood well enough or widely enough to have led to lasting solutions. Herein lies the mission for this book. Solving any problem begins by attempting to understand it. And understanding, in this case, requires us to dissect, characterize, and analyze the length and breadth of our human problems and the terrain of society in which they are set.

Broadly, this book is a primer on the factors and forces that shape human society. Building on this foundation, and using it as a springboard, the deeper focus and aim is to search out the specific cultural features that have the most to say about the challenges facing our world today.

To my thinking, the best way to analyze society is as a system—because that is what it is: a logical maze of causes and effects that both lead to and explain the cultural outcomes we see around us. It is the "moving parts" to this system that make up the main content of these chapters.

The aspect of social dynamics that we will concentrate on is corruption. People in the know say that we are fast approaching what may be our last chance here on Earth to "get it right," given a half dozen or more collapse or decline scenarios that have been identified. If corruption within government and other social institutions plays a role in this state of affairs, then hopefully we will hit pay dirt with this focus.

So what does corruption mean for society, and who is corrupt? We are concerned with two specific things. First, there is a divide between individuals who act with the common good in mind, and those who act exclusively for their own self-gain. This latter behavior can be considered to be antisocial, and is at odds with the spirit and intent of a democracy. The ascension of this personality type to powerful positions in society is one component of what I am calling "corruption." The second aspect of corruption that will concern us is a potential gross concentration of power or wealth in relatively few hands. It is correct to believe that consolidated power can distort or undermine a democracy. What may not be as well understood is just how that circumstance can come about. Addressing the details of when and why power concentrates is a unifying thread in this book and frames a conundrum that we will flesh out and attempt to solve.

One theme in these pages begins with the simple idea that everything in culture originates with the actions of a someone or somebody. If we are looking for solutions to problems, this means we can start by following any one of them back to find which individual— or individuals—may have contributed to creating it. Some human problems trace to an inadequacy of information, some to a breakdown in communication, some to a failure of imagination. But at the far end of the great majority of them is someone for whom it is not a problem at all—someone who is willfully gaining from their actions and who, more often than not, has a disproportionate amount of power and influence.

Instead of considering specific solutions to identified problems, I will be working one step removed, concentrating on what can be thought of as the solutions that enable the solutions—a twist of phrase that will become clear as we go forward.

It is hoped that this combined focus can lend clarity to the complex questions facing humanity, and that it can work, as well, to heighten people's attention to, or personal involvement in, the puzzle of how to finally create a just and life-enhancing society that is enduring.

I will be using the word "elite" to refer to the wealthiest and most powerful subculture in society—usually meaning in a Western society. It could be said to be synonymous with the "1 percent" or perhaps the "0.1 percent." True, people in any segment of society deserve not to be given a simplifying label that misses the fact of their actual diversity. It is certainly a theme of this book that the world is made up of individuals, and not of categories of people. For brevity of prose, however, my use of "elite" sometimes cuts this corner. I ask the reader to stretch a little to know this is the case. And it is hard to find the perfect word for the *opposite* of the elite. The 99 percent, the public, the populace, the citizenry, all can pass and will have to do. These are some of the terms I use to designate the balance of society that is not in the highest echelon of wealth or influence.

The word "democracy" I use loosely to refer to a social system in which people have an approximately equal say in the managing of their government—where there is, in other words, a relatively equal distribution of both political and economic power.

My style of discourse, as you will see, could remind one of a skipping stone—barely touching down before moving on. In part, the presentation is meant to be a long string of starting points: starting points for conversation, for brainstorming, for debate, for planning.

Chapter One

The Logic of Social Systems

The greatest "Aha!" moment of my life was the day I first encountered the idea of self-organization. Outside of human activity, I learned, nearly everything that is known to exist has, essentially, created itself. This is extraordinary! Solar systems and galaxies structure themselves; atomic nuclei self-assemble in stars; organisms make themselves—lock, stock, and barrel—from raw materials; the earth's crust raises, lowers, and rearranges itself; the atmosphere self-sorts into layers; and on and on. Remarkably, I also learned, this is all done with just four known fundamental forces—two of which are confined to the nucleus of the atom. Almost everything that is chemistry, including life, is driven by positive charges and negative charges acting within and between atoms. Almost everything geologic, in contrast, is mediated by the gravitational force acting between objects with mass. Celestial order includes a major role for gravity and additional roles for nuclear reactions and electro-magnetic activity. The phenomena that we are surrounded by can all be traced back to objects or agents—microscopic and macroscopic—interacting via forces. Everything that comes into being in the natural world happens, in effect, spontaneously, from the bottom up, of its own accord.

With the one significant addition of a top-down component, human culture can be understood using the exact same approach: agents or objects interacting via forces. In a social system—such as a community, nation, or the world itself—individual humans are the agents, and the rules we follow when we act are those of our psychology. We interact with each other and with the broader environment, and the phantasmagoria of human culture emerges.

A goal of this book is to try to gain a better understanding of human culture by analyzing it as a self-organizing system. Putting this analysis directly to work, there are problems that need solving. Humans are known to act in ways that can adversely affect other humans, other organisms in the biosphere, and future generations of both. Familiar social, political, international, and environmental challenges still beg for our concerted attention or for properly reasoned responses. In the pages ahead we will attempt to puzzle out solutions to these and other concerns. One thesis we will explore is the idea that many or most of the world's problems trace to an unequal distribution of power, and that that inequality is a direct outcome of easily identifiable patterns in social systems.

In addition to building on theory to understand society, it is important to decipher where we currently stand in the United States on the spectrum between liberty and its antithesis, usually labeled as tyranny. Devising effective ideas for reform or social change depends on knowing what the starting point is. What I have come to believe is that we are at the eleventh hour in a struggle to save at least our democracy and, potentially, civilization itself. I am proposing that we are in an advanced stage of corruption in the US—an idea that is familiar to many. There are no technological fixes for this kind of problem and no magic nostrums to simply set things right. Instead, there is the authentic work of engaging the subject with our intellects and turning our ideas into actions. One source for conceptual and analytic tools to use in coming to grips with this suggested challenge is the social and behavioral sciences, which we will tap in an effort to identify the most salient patterns and processes at work in the culture around us. Making sense of any given system means identifying and understanding the logic of the interaction of its component parts. And that is how we will begin.

Build a model

Nature has no particular reason to parcel her creations into discrete systems with obvious dividing lines between them. It is left to us to choose the most useful way to frame a given system in order to learn about it. This is true, as well, for probing the outcome of human behaviors. Here, in the following paragraphs, I describe a rudimentary model of culture to use as a basis for the discussion ahead.

Culture is the product of the collective action of willful humans. We define culture here as every consequence of the expression of our will through the use of our muscles. Culture, therefore, includes all voluntary human behaviors and all human-created artifacts. It encompasses everything we do and everything we create. True, it could seem natural for thoughts themselves to be a part of culture, particularly as they encode ideas. But no thought enters or joins culture to be interacted with until it is translated into action. Ideas and thoughts are embedded in an elaborately populated mental environment and form a discrete system that is natural to evaluate in its own right. A computer analogy describes a suggested layout perfectly: Our bodies, using our muscles, are the output devices which generate culture. Our minds are the CPU (central processing unit), operating system, applications software, and memory. The full array of our senses become the input devices, channeling information about our environment into our bodies to be "processed." Culture, through all of the means by which we perceive it, then becomes an input—helping dictate future outputs. And we're off! Culture, therefore, is made up of books, bridges, smartphones, meeting minutes, YouTube videos, our body language, a dance, the sounds we create, and the aroma wafting from a restaurant. Machines are culture, and when we run them, what they do is a part of culture. This is an unorthodox definition for culture but has many advantages, including that it makes everything in culture a tangible, and even measurable, thing.

Define power

Our naturally selected behavior apparatus is what guides us in deciding how to act. At every turn, we can say, we are acting to increase our well-being. This is the equivalent to the economists' utility. Well-being can be considered to be our perpetual goal and seeking it our composite motivator. But, somewhat ironically, long-term gains in it are negligible. Well-being tends to reset in such a way that most of us are forever striving, irrespective of our successes—a set-up that happens to make good sense as an evolutionary adaptation. As well-being goes up and down, it has relatively little effect on our individual behavior.

So, as the economic or social status of individuals in society changes, what, if anything, does grow or shrink significantly? One answer is that our ability to shape or influence the world around us will vary greatly. This is our power. We can be powerless or be powerful as life circumstance dictates. Here we define power as a quantitative measure of our ability to influence the physical or cultural environment in which we live. Variability in power comes from differences in innate intelligence, acquired knowledge, drive, creativity, physical appearance (such as attractiveness), and physical capability (such as brawn or agility). Greater power enables a person to be proactive instead of reactive or to have many choices instead of few. It helps a person manifest things that they wish for for themselves or others.

A defining quality of democratic governance is that all people have approximately equal political power. From this point of view, if one person had more power in a democracy, you could argue that someone else would consequently have less. This feature of power is true in many arenas. For this reason we will consider the distribution of power in a social system to be zero-sum.

Vectors / forces

Everything in culture and society, as we have said, is created by humans. There is nothing other than *somebody* that brings any cultural thing into existence. Our actions can be visualized as forces and talked about in much the same way a physicist describes forces—having both a direction and a magnitude. The direction relates to *what* we are seeking, while the magnitude is the power we have with which to pursue it. My use of the word "forces" in describing human activity in society reflects this kind of meaning.

How we choose to act in each moment is determined by our psychology. Sometimes consciously, sometimes unconsciously, we are forever making cost-benefit assessments of the choices available to us. This is a distinctly environment-dependent thing. We face different choices with different pros and cons in each environment we find ourselves in. I use the word "environment" here in the broadest sense to include the natural and cultural setting within which we live and make choices. The notion of a cost-benefit "calculation" for making choices in life will be familiar to many as what is called rational choice theory.

We spoke above about top-down features of culture. It is not always easy to tease apart the difference between bottom-up and top-down phenomena. Generally, any time there is a process that is codified in order to be followed or repeated it can be thought of as a top-down module. Culture is full of top-down processes that humans have created. Examples include a blueprint, recipe, constitution, musical score, and our traffic rules. In contrast to the expected outcome from following such prescriptions, something that, instead, generates novelty through the acting of active agents means there are bottom-up processes at work.

Only when a self-organizing system with interacting active agents starts to "run" do its characteristics begin to emerge. Human social organization has been running for easily 50,000 years. In that time it has evolved to and through a fantastic range of incarnations, each of which, in their time and place, fit within the context and trajectory of a particular culture. This historical diversity mirrors a remarkable feature of biological systems. Given what one would think of as a strict bottom line—that of producing offspring that survive to produce offspring—there is, for some good reason, an enormous number of versions of how organisms succeed at succeeding. In the realm of reproduction, for example, there is every imaginable permutation of how who courts and selects whom, to make one or a million offspring, that are reared, or not, according to each species' time-tested approach. It is a good precedent for us to observe that so many possibilities can all be viable. There is no fear of a deterministic fate for humans. The sky is the limit, as long as we do not paint ourselves into the proverbial corner before we have time to sort out our current difficulties.

System behavior

Tracking and analyzing the details of culture that emerge through time falls to a range of academic disciplines. The field of systems theory and the closely related complexity theory are two that offer tools, concepts, and framework for understanding and discussing culture. A cook's tour of systems theory would include an introduction to the following: tipping points and critical mass; positive, negative, and chaotic feedbacks; sensitive dependence on initial conditions; attractors; oscillating states; non-feedback evolution or migration; and sorting behaviors. Many of these have something important to contribute to elucidating features of human culture. We will describe several of them here, and go on to utilize most of them in the pages ahead.

Feedback

The term "feedback" almost explains itself. When an outcome of a process circles back to influence the same process, there is feedback. If an output becomes a new input, it can enhance a trend such that more becomes more, or less becomes less. This is called positive feedback. When an output circles to become an input it can also stabilize a given value, where more leads to less, leads to more, leads to less. This is called negative, or stabilizing, feedback. Positive feedback augments something, while negative feedback leads to a leveling off. The field of geology offers a neat example of both: Positive feedback, via water erosion, leads to steep mountains with deep valleys, while negative feedback, via deposition of sediments, leads to flat landscapes, floodplains, and the smooth geometry of alluvial fans.

Human culture is replete with examples of both positive and negative feedback. When there is no feedback in a social system, human actions and their consequences ripple outward in a linear chain of events—one causing the next, causing the next—like a Rube Goldberg contraption. When feedback does exist, it can be weak or strong, and be either immediate or delayed.

Animal populations exhibit a form of negative feedback whereby the better a population does, the worse it does, and the worse it does, the better it does. In this dynamic, if the size of a population of a given organism grows, then there is less of its food to go around, meaning the population may subsequently shrink. At the same time, a larger population means there are more of that organism available to be eaten by—and thereby build the populations of—their predators. A population will swell and shrink in a delayed response to both its predator and prey (including plant) populations. This is classic negative feedback and, as illustrated here, will function to stabilize a given something at, or around, a certain value. One could argue that the number of cars on the road follows this frequency-dependent pattern. If traffic is heavy, then people notice and—instead of driving—they will choose to stay home, walk, bicycle, or take public transportation. The amount of traffic then goes down. With traffic being lighter, people again notice, and choose to drive more often.

In economics, speculative bubbles are a textbook positive feedback example: Buying in to a trending item sends up the price, which attracts yet more buyers, who send it up further. It would also be positive feedback when the bubble bursts: the more a price plunges, the more sellers will cause it to plunge.

A sometimes all-too-familiar example of positive feedback in our lives is the fact of people standing up at sports events or rock concerts. If everyone at such an event stayed seated, everyone would be able to see. But if one person stands, others may follow, and a chain reaction ensues. Unfortunately for shorter people, heights are more variable when we stand than when we sit! A party or gathering that is turning out to be a "dud" also exhibits positive feedback: the more people leave, the more people will tend to leave. A party that is "happening" follows the same positive feedback reasoning in reverse.

A system has two choices: it can be evolving and changing, or it can be stable and not changing (in a given time frame). If a system is stable, it can be static like a rock on the ground, or it can be dynamic, with shifting values. If it is stable but dynamic, then it is the logic of negative feedback that holds it steadily within certain bounds. A prerequisite to the viability of life is its ability to maintain this kind of dynamic equilibrium. Virtually every aspect of the metabolism of an organism includes negative feedback mechanisms that regulate the level of important molecules. This negative feedback is the product of the "design" ability of natural selection. Many systems that are evolving and changing will naturally find their way into patterns which then stabilize them. Humans have the ability to intentionally design something such that it has a built-in stability. Goals for social change could include finding acceptable equilibrium points for such things as the distribution of wealth.

Sometimes positive feedback is strong enough that it locks in one, and only one, outcome. This is similar to what, in economics, is called a natural monopoly. In such cases two different versions of a product, service, or protocol will not, usually, both exist. Examples include the shirt-buttoning conventions for men and women, an optical disc format, or the side of the road we drive on. It would be inefficient—or worse—to have more than one version of these things. This pattern can apply to information in the public sphere in that we are uncomfortable living with mutually exclusive facts. To the extent to which we hear news about the world that turns out to be completely wrong, it may be due to information lock-in by the party whose account of things initially won out.

Sorting

One thing a system can "do" is to sort by some criteria. By being mobile and willful and different from each other, humans have all the requirements to self-sort in multiple ways. A baker, for example, might do best to set up shop as far away from competitors as possible, leading to a wide and even distribution of bakeries. Likewise with many other services and products. Some businesses, on the other hand, find that their search for market share is best served when they are clustered, as with fast food chain stores. Some criteria spread us out, while other criteria work to concentrate us. Our choosing of a region, town, and neighborhood in which to live builds demographic patterns. Usually humans sort themselves by seeking sameness: same cultural background, same tolerance for a hot or cold climate, same religious beliefs. Individuals who, in contrast, identify difference and newness with pleasure, will seek out diversity, choosing "other" over "same," and creating more mixing in the process.

Sorting preferences can dovetail with feedback loops. If an urban neighborhood is tending toward an upscale revitalization, this can build on itself as a new set of businesses and residents move in and encourage more of the same. A neighborhood can tip in directions based on things such as ethnicity, income level, or age. If an outcome seems certain, then positive feedback will seal it—at least for the time being.

Attractors

In several of these examples there are states that a societal system will be drawn to by one positive feedback mechanism or another. These states are what can be called "attractors," and pictured as if they were gravitational fields. Logic will draw a dynamic system like society towards the most likely attractors—if there are any. A tipping point or critical mass is like entering such a gravitational field: it is the edge of an attractor and path to a new state. As the concept goes, the motion is inevitable—until negative feedback stabilizes it, or some other factor changes. The technical definition of an attractor requires that if something is perturbed, it will restore itself.

Most people would agree that the challenges currently facing humanity are monumental. Many of our problems are longstanding or intractable, with a few too new to fully grasp. These range from internecine conflicts, economic exploitation, wars of aggression, environmental illnesses, and widespread poverty to water shortages, threats of tyranny, climate change, radioactive contamination, and an increasingly pauperized biosphere—to name just a few. Given that the theory of natural selection says we evolved to be (by a strict definition) selfish, it is not unreasonable to think that greed, the profit motive, or selfishness generally, are at the root of these issues. I would like, however, to approach the question of the status of our civilization from a different point of view. Regardless of how individual humans may or may not act, what if a feature of the behavior of society as a system could be named as the most telling aspect of our human circumstance? What if a society based on equality is not a stable system, and *inequality* is an attractor toward which social systems will naturally move? And further, what if that inequality, and an *absence* of democracy, is the source of the majority of humanity's problems?

Power divergence

As a thought experiment, imagine if everyone in the world were given an equal share of wealth. This would resemble the optimistic founding of a democratic republic with its equal political power as the intended starting point. What would then happen to wealth distribution, and the concomitant power balance, as time passed? If we were to add almost any element of human variability—such as differences in aptitude, scruples, or motivation—into this picture, it is almost certain that some divergence in the distribution of wealth would begin. And what if individuals who began to gain an edge in wealth were able to use that edge to gain yet more wealth? This could start a positive feedback loop in which more begets more begets more—while, relatively, less begets less. The end result of this repeating cycle will be a society with a disproportionately wealthy and powerful subculture. Since that subculture could eventually have free rein to tailor even the government to its wishes, then all is lost for the experimental egalitarian society. This is the one-minute version of this storyline. Close inspection, as we will see, reveals a multitude of potential pathways for such a cyclical concentration and consolidation of wealth and power.

The simplest scenario that leads to a divergence in wealth can be illustrated with several bank accounts that earn interest at the same rate but begin with different amounts of money. If the interest is compounding, each account will grow by a percentage of itself. The amounts will double in the same length of time. So in the time it takes for $100 to become $200, $200 has become $400—and one million dollars has become two million dollars. These are each growing via the same rules, yet one or another can grow to become relatively huge through an initial advantage.

Power, as we have said, is a measure of the ability we each have to influence the world around us. While it can be based on intelligence, knowledge, charisma, or motivation, the thing that often equates most closely with power is money or wealth. The more money one has, the easier it is to make big plans and carry them out. You can use money to get education that furthers opportunity for advancement. You can use it to hire people to help you fulfill your dreams or ambitions. Money and wealth can often be a shorthand measure of an individual's power.

Two academic specialties that have much to contribute to understanding the dynamics and outcomes of human interactions are game theory and what is called agent-based modeling (ABM). Because of the complexity of real cultural processes, investigators often find it most illuminating to craft simplified and carefully defined "games" that model specific aspects of culture. When devising a game scenario to analyze and illustrate a human interaction, game theorists assign payoffs to the winners and losers to mirror a realistic situation. A game may be iterated, repeating itself with the same players while keeping score. This game-constructing approach can be used to perfectly illustrate how a form of feedback can lead to power accumulation. Payoffs to the winner in a realistic "game of society" could include the ability to change a future rule of the game and/or change the behavior of other players—both potentially leading to a position of advantage. Repetition of this game cycle clearly could deepen the entrenchment of a winning player. The consequence of these two particular payoffs would not be unlike what we witness in society today, as the "game board" is progressively altered by winners who also are able to engage in shaping the behavior of their fellow citizens.

In the preceding paragraphs the two scenarios that illustrate divergence in wealth or power are 1) a difference in initial conditions (the bank accounts) and 2) using winnings to change the game. The difference in initial conditions, incidentally, can also be looked at as if certain players had a head start. In the next chapter we will introduce and explore other dynamics that influence power accumulation, deepening the theme that social equality may be a precarious or vulnerable state that is inherently difficult to achieve or maintain.

With the collapse of the Soviet Union in 1991, political commentators in the US had made a point of declaring that socialism lost out to democracy—proving who had the superior system. The true winner in that longstanding ideological drama, however, was neither of these two contestants. There is great irony in US elites stating that democracy has prevailed in the world, since they, as a subculture, appear to be as opposed to the equality of democracy as they have been to the equality associated with socialism. Democracy and socialism actually have much in common. Socialism, by aiming for a classless society, tries to eliminate the corrupting effect of imbalances in wealth, while democracy promotes equality of political power as the formula for a good society. Both are about equality—one economic, the other political—and both are, arguably, unstable systems. The real story may be that these kinds of experiments in equality have tended to fail for the same reason: they are prone to corrupting patterns that concentrate wealth and power. The details of what prevails in society may turn out to have less to do with virtue, per se, and more to do with the logic of contests and systems.

The not-surprising reason the elite have had to oppose an equality of wealth or political power is that equality means sharing things, like resources, that they otherwise would have the power not to share. If they are winning hands down at accumulating power and wealth, why would they choose to support a system that undermined that advantage? This opposition to equality has been amply demonstrated by US foreign policy over many decades. Experiments in democracy have, in fact, been attacked as fiercely as experiments in socialism. During the Cold War in particular, elites had pretended to be fighting a bad-guy version of socialism, while instead fighting movements for self-determination that usually happily model themselves after the ideals of Western democracies.

What is

The most basic question one can ask about any given thing in the universe is, "What accounts for it being there for us to witness in the first place?" Assuming there are an untold number of alternatives that could exist, why *this* particular thing—why here and why now? Behind all phenomena and all outcomes there is a story or narrative, an explanation that makes sense of the origin and existence of what is. Cultural phenomena and outcomes all have their stories and explanations as well. Using our model of society as a self-organizing system, humans are the indivisible agents whose actions perpetually bring new cultural things into existence. From here, the logic of a very complex system kicks in. Of the many things we each strive for, only some come to pass. Of the many things we actualize, only certain of these go on to survive, persist, or become predominant—while others do not.

Across the span of culture there is a winnowing, or selection, down from what could exist, to what does exist.

The logic of what survives, or what wins, can be as complex as that of a chess game, as certain players are indeed strategizing with exactly that degree of sophistication. The explanations for what survives can also be surprising. For example, you could make the argument that every time a white-collar crime shows up in the headlines, it is one more scheme that was not clever enough to survive—thereby leaving intact only the cleverest. The surviving outcomes in culture can include both winners *and* losers, as the prevalence of poverty illustrates.

Fads and fashions survive and can have the life cycle they do because of a logic not unlike the rise and fall of stock prices. When something is rare or novel, it has the potential to be a status item that distinguishes the individual who has it. With the proper jumpstart the item can grow in popularity by positive feedback (the more it is seen, the more it is adopted) until its very abundance destroys the cutting-edge association, it enters "has been" status, and plummets in popularity.

Cultural novelty, unlike most new variation in the attributes of organisms, is not generated by a random process. Variation in culture is usually invented with a purpose in mind. Ideas are hatched in order to fulfill a need, solve a problem, or grow an enterprise—all willed. In addition, culture and its propagation includes a great deal of copying and variation on themes, with the obvious sense that this makes and the advantages it yields.

When contemplating what survives, think also of the things that do not survive, such as the corkscrew that was too confusing, clothing styles that didn't catch on, the restaurant too out of the way to be noticed, NGOs that ran out of money, or political candidates who were not elected. Culture changes perpetually to be populated with the features that are the most likely to first exist, and then persist.

Things that align with the orientation of the most powerful groupings in society will tend to emerge, survive, and flourish under their stewardship, while things that run contrary to the interests of such individuals will tend to be weeded out. These players have the capacity to influence the costs and benefits of choices throughout society, steering the behavior of their fellow citizens through a range of temptations, enticements, and opportunities, as well as disincentives. Movements, enterprises, governments, and ideas can be vanquished in the course of this winnowing dynamic. Heavy-handed actions by powerful people may directly impact the survival of certain things by, for instance, controlling funding, discrediting individuals, buying out competing ventures, or overthrowing foreign leaders. In certain cases fear leads to more cautious life choices with the cumulative impact that has on the makeup of culture.

Cultural inventions that address powerful human needs or desires can be expected to be present cross-culturally in one form or another through time. Our love of sport—like the play behavior of so many animals—is a need that is wired to hunting and other longstanding primal activities. Anything that taps into our body's capacity for psychological or physical pleasure will likewise be a magnet for cultural inventiveness, including to do with food, intoxicants, sensuality, and sexuality.

Social Darwinism

Posing questions about what survives, while discussing culture, can't help but bring to mind the phrase social Darwinism. The most familiar meaning for this term suggests that individuals who prosper in society do so because of innate virtues such as strength of character or intelligence, and that their survival or success establishes that they were the "fittest." The idea that the people or things that prevail in society are the best has been used at various times to promote laissez-faire (hands-off) style economics as a means for allowing virtues, and virtuous individuals, to flourish. It has also been invoked historically to ennoble (or embolden) nations that subdued other lands and peoples. But if individuals, or even countries, prosper because they are the fittest, what is it that they are the fittest at? The answer, of course, is that they are the fittest at merely prevailing or winning, which by itself may not be anything to be proud of. It is true, there are plenty of admirable or virtuous characteristics that lead individuals to prosper in society. Intelligence, for example, facilitates mastery of many arcane things in our complex modern world and can earn wealth and high social status for a person. But there are also many vices, such as ruthless business practices—not to mention barbarity—that can correlate with prominence or success.

Darwinism itself makes no value judgment. Evolution by natural selection, while historically misunderstood to equate with progress and improvement is, instead, primarily about the match that organisms have with their environment. Biologists matter-of-factly work to decipher why that which survives in nature does survive. Our analysis of what survives in culture will likewise be scientific, objective, and value-free. By contrast with the *explanation* for features of culture, a discussion on how to create a better world—which we also undertake here—is all about subjectivity. A "problem" is a subjective thing, while the facts of how the circumstances of it arose are facts alone.

It is universal in civilized culture to make judgments on behavior. This is what our laws are. Likewise, some declaration of ethical standards, and of good and bad, seems to be necessary and appropriate

for a conversation about the future of society. To a first approxima-
tion I would say that it is ethical to be conscious of, and willing to
act toward, the common good, and it is unethical to not.

A notion of survival of the fittest, applied to what survives culturally, can be a useful idea as long as value judgments are set aside,
"fittest" is clarified, and there is an appreciation that the logic of what
survives is a complex matter. Elites may see society as a meritocracy
in which they deserve the power they have because they have earned
it through hard work and superior ability. In response to this perspective, I hope to make it clear that the elite may have achieved
what they have, in part, through advantages in the logic of wealth
accumulation, which itself may include unethical practices. The
processes we will identify that shape and govern the makeup of culture will not necessarily lead naturally to the "best of all possible
worlds." Our speculation, to the contrary, is that a concentration and
subsequent abuse of power is almost a law of nature, and that preventing or reversing this outcome would depend on a focused and
concerted collective effort by the public.

It is reasonable to ask why, if nature has no right and wrong, and
the law of the jungle has worked for *it*, should there need to be anything different for society? There may be many answers to this question, but one is simply that nature is too cruel to be emulated. We
need and can easily create a better model for ourselves.

Selection pressure

One more idea that it is useful to borrow from the biological sciences is the notion of selection pressure. When a given capability or
attribute of an organism in nature is highly consequential, selection
pressure on it is high. If a capability or attribute has little consequence, then there is low selection pressure. In nature, selection pressure dictates the urgency of refining an adaptation. In culture, as we

have been emphasizing, there is what would be called "differential survival" of the things that we create: some survive, some do not. It is a cultural version of selection pressure that determines how strong this weeding-out is along the way, and how important the ongoing refinement of something is. In California there is strong cultural selection pressure for building structures that are earthquake-proof. In Iowa there is weak pressure for this same trait or feature. In some towns the pressure is acute for a restaurant or other storefront business to succeed. In other towns a halfhearted effort could exist for decades. This is similar to how much competition there is in a market.

Forces at work

It is true enough that the explanation for many things in society is highly complex and includes the hard-to-predict outcomes of what are called nonlinear processes. But there is much that can be understood by the simple adding up of forces, as with the physicist's vectors we described earlier. Using the idea that every psychology-driven action is a force with a direction and a magnitude, we can piece together the composite factors behind certain small and large developments in society.

As an illustration of this accounting process, we can look at the forces that affect the emergence of war. Because wars come into existence through human actions, we can look for what are, essentially, incentives or rewards that lead individuals to act in ways that either contribute to war, or counteract it.

If you, for example, were an arms manufacturer, you would most likely attempt to influence the world around you to create more buyers for your product. If you did not, then another arms manufacturer probably would, acquiring more market share for themselves in the process.

If you were a career military planner, you might want to apply your elaborate plans to a real-life situation and satisfy a natural need for validation.

What if you were a banker and the more money you were able to lend, the more money you made? If wars and their aftermath presented opportunities for lending, would your professional actions contribute to creating or maintaining war?

Eager and curious munitions designers themselves provide a force toward war as advances in technology lure them onward to design and test new weapons.

Human motivation will take some forms that are not readily apparent. Forward-thinking planners may identify things such as a rare mineral, essential to a given technology, as the non-negotiable reason to invade a country.

For certain businesses, the longer a war goes on, the more money can be made. In some cases every missile fired means another missile ordered.

A full-fledged racket could emerge in which it was profitable to sell arms to two countries, encourage them to fight each other, then lend them money to rebuild, using your contractors.

If you were one of the above interested parties and also had a stake in a media conglomerate, would you use the persuasive power of that media to promote military solutions to problems or exaggerate the threat of an adversary?

A search for incentives leads to the question of where the money for war comes from. Government is usually the largest spender in an economy. The government capacity for spending would initially represent a market opportunity or, in ecological terms, an unexploited niche. There would logically be many groups acting in a full range of industries to try to get government to preferentially service their wishes. Using the idea of cultural selection pressure, the larger the potential payout to interested parties, the stronger the lobbying and other advocacy for a "cause" would be. Other than space exploration, it is hard to imagine a more costly endeavor than war. On top of this, a psychologically compelling rationale like the security of the nation in a dangerous world would add significant weight to the "selling" of a large military to the public and hence to the government. There are forces, in other words, toward war spending by government, that are not necessarily because of a need for war, but because it is both lucrative and an easy endeavor to promote. This may seem like a stretch of reasoning but is no more than the familiar boondoggle on a large scale. In the case where a democracy has succumbed to control by an overly powerful minority, government spending can be seen, in part, as a vehicle for transferring money from public to private hands—here, facilitated by a militarized culture.

The single easiest way to gain wealth is to merely take it from someone—if you can get away with it. The resources of another country (or whole continent, such as Africa) are a temptation to those powerful enough to arrange to have them. In some cases a war can be seen as a heist. It has been the norm in history that if you conquer something, then it is yours. This precedent and presumption may be in the process of changing, or simply becoming subtler. The payoff to private interests of getting a government to work on your behalf to secure exploitation opportunities is enormous. Trying to gain access to a resource the honest way becomes a seemingly naive alternative if you are a Goliath.

If these forces, in the form of individual actions that contribute to war, were only additive, this could still be a sizable resulting force. More realistic, however, is that they act to create a self-reinforcing snowball effect as the profits from war lead to individuals with the power to direct the country to more militarization and war. Augmenting this, networks of individuals and institutions set up naturally when their interests come into alignment.

Wars, of course, also happen because of historic rivalries, misunderstandings, differing perceptions of justice, and psychological motivators such as fear and honor. These can each provide their own vectors that lead toward military preparedness or to war itself. Defense against an aggressor, ironically, means that an otherwise disinclined country might have to create their own military, derailing the peacetime application of the same resources.

There are also players who act to prevent war. Advocates for justice contribute a force against unjust wars. Costs to citizens in terms of dollars, as well as life and limb, can sometimes mean they are a counterforce. Rationales like mutually assured destruction provide a disincentive, at least for tangling with an equally powerful adversary.

A matter-of-fact answer to why a war exists is that if there are enough forces and factors that push toward it—and not enough pushing against it—then war will happen.

A familiar form of public soul-searching, and of commentary on our national and global predicaments, refers to the need for a collective "we" or "us" to learn to do things differently. "Time is running out for us to change our profligate ways," for example. Though it is important to acknowledge our individual role in the complex web of culture, it is a mistake to neglect the true play of forces behind issues of the day. Something that we refer to as "our" problem may actually be a bonanza for certain individuals who could be the selfsame people most responsible for creating it in the first place. This is cui bono writ large, and is a sensible way to proceed in understanding the anatomy of an identified problem.

We have begun to describe how unequal power distribution can be a state toward which a society will gravitate. The more accurate qualification we use from here on in is that inequality will tend to exist under certain circumstances, just as equality will exist under its own sets of circumstances. Every potential outcome in society will depend on the setting, on the context, on the environment. This helps us frame the challenge of how to respond to a full range of societal issues. We can ask, for example, "What kind of environment will foster, or lead to, outcome A, versus outcome B?"

An extraordinary thing about our moment in history is that answers to the most pressing questions facing humanity are not that hard to find. Everything we have presented so far is common sense with a few frills. Yet hopefully this orientation is sufficient to set us on track to better understand a number of pivotal dynamics in society, including the role that expressions of power have in either the failure or fulfillment of a democratic vision.

CHAPTER TWO

Dynamics That Shape Society

As culture is created by the actions and interactions of humans, patterns emerge, some of which recur as signature features of our social systems, and all of which present opportunities for insight into how society works. On eleven different topics, what follows is a collection of patterns of logic—of causes and their effects, small and large—that can be found in the fabric of the society around us. They have been chosen for the light they shed on both the problem of corruption and the promise of reclaiming a fair and just social order. Recall that the two expressions of corruption we are treating as most important are first, when power has become highly concentrated and second, when power is in the hands of immoral or ethically compromised people. Concentrated power skews the spirit of democracy, and unethical behavior is destructive of, and incompatible with, a just and peaceful society. The two combined can wreak havoc.

Remember, also, that we are interested in identifying how and why things come to exist as they do in society. The first and most general kind of explanation is that things exist because humans choose them, or create them, to fulfill a need or desire. The kind of reasoning behind why certain things then persist or go on to become predominant is part of what is explored in each of these sections.

1　The Power Conundrum

The world is in the midst of a renaissance of social engagement and activism. Though the percentage of individuals involved in this may be small, their creativity and dedication is not. Discussions about social change are brimming with ideas that, if implemented, would have a profound positive impact on our world. Some of these initiatives can and do take hold. Some do so via market forces as consumers change their views and support alternatives. A few innovative proposals make their way through a legislative process to become laws that create beneficial incentives or accountability. But the majority of these good ideas simply will not earn the chance to be tried and evaluated if there is not the power with which to do so. This takes us to a meta level of social change: the change required for the change.

The problem of disempowerment can be posed as an infinite regress. To effect change, we need the power and influence to do so. But we can't gain that crucial power and influence without more power and influence than we have. And how do we get that? Well, only with power and with influence.

This presents us with a puzzle and a threat. First, how can the logic of this pattern be altered or challenged to effectively recoup waning influence both in government and over our lives? And second, what happens if a seeming lock on power and influence by those who have it cannot be broken?

As we began to explore in Chapter One, if power, under certain circumstances, can be used to gain more power, then once a divergence in power gets started within a democracy, it could theoretically grow and continue to grow—even exponentially. It should be true that the checks and balances of a healthy democracy can intercede in a timely way to maintain a distribution of power within certain bounds. But if there were positive feedback in the gaining of power (in which the more you had, the more you could get), there is probably also a point beyond which growing inequality cannot be checked or rectified. What might this point of no return be, and would we recognize it if faced with it? Is there a reason to think we are near to such a point in the US today? Have we passed it, and is our fate sealed?

This frames a conundrum. It takes power to get the power to gain in power—and it takes power to take power away from those who, arguably, have too much. How can a population with dwindling power escape from this bind in order to restore a relative equality of influence in its society? If we are proposing that most of the world's problems have to do with a lack of real democracy—with an inability of people to advocate adequately for their own welfare—then this question is an important one.

Power, you will remember, we defined as a measure of our ability to influence the world around us. Power equates closely with wealth, since money can be used to accomplish or to create a great range of things. But, fortunately, power also equates with knowledge, social skills, and certain personality traits, as well as with gumption and inspiration, which help propel our actions. Power can be strategically pooled. It can also be won or lost on the reputation or public image of the players. These, among other factors, can be drawn from to counter consolidated or misused power. This is good news.

Our primary theme here—and the reasoning behind it—may be broader than just a summation of the current predicament in a struggling US democracy. A case can be made that the most consequential single dynamic in all of human history is that the acquisition of power follows positive feedback logic. The percentage of history that involves the domination of one group by another is substantial. We will, at least, fully plumb this idea for its relevance to today's social concerns.

2 Changing the Playing Field

In one simple phrase the words "level playing field" sum up the notion of what fairness in politics or an economy could look like. We
talked in the previous chapter about the capacity of winners in a
game to change rules in their favor. A playing field analogy works
just as well to help illustrate the idea that fairness is something that
can be eroded, including by processes that feed back and are cyclical,
enabling some humans to progressively create an environment in
which they themselves thrive.

The playing field of society encompasses the state of the job market, the strength of civil liberties, the affordability of health care, and
the status of labor rights. It includes whether there is a reliably fair
election process, whether a person's pension or Social Security is secure, and whether or not a citizen has a guarantee of due process
under the law. The playing field is the laws of the land, the structure
of the economy, the state of the marketplace. An aspect of the playing
field is the "menu" of options people have to choose from. Higher
education can be free in one era and cost $200,000 in another, sharply
influencing life choices. The shape of the playing field—whether it
is level or otherwise—is determined collectively by us, and the more
power someone has, the larger a role he or she can play in influencing
it. Systems-thinking pioneer, Donella Meadows, says that system
structure is the source of system behavior. Changing the playing field
involves changing system structure.

In society, advantageous changes to the playing field could have
outcomes that look like the following: If you succeed at influencing
congressional appropriations, your company can have access to no-
bid contracts. If you hire lobbyists to help pass the right legislation,
your economic sector can be subsidized by taxpayers. If you can
arrange to massage investment ratings, a system ripe for gaming is
at your fingertips. If your media corporation can sell the right can-

didates to the public, you can change laws restricting media acquisitions. If you have control over search engine algorithms, you can lead people to find what you want them to find and not find what you don't. If you change the right rules of finance and banking, there are suddenly new niches to exploit. If you can influence patent law, then you can get monopoly rights to something that would otherwise be un-patentable or remain in the public domain. If your business can be freed from the threat of lawsuits, your financial risk is sharply diminished. Depending on what is your cup of tea—and your leverage—you can use power to change tax laws, arrange to be bailed out, drive competitors out of business, or legalize an otherwise illegal activity.

Powerful people have the chance to determine who is at the head of colleges, universities, the CDC, the EPA, NATO, the WTO, as well as who holds federal and state court and cabinet positions—shaping the policies that emanate from these institutions or agencies. Hierarchical structures maximize the influence of such appointments. By creating foundations, people with great wealth can institutionalize their financial support for ventures that match their values and objectives.

Changing the playing field changes the costs and the benefits of behaviors and, with that, changes the choices people make. The status of the playing field can mean it costs more to do good, or that there are additional temptations to do bad. Something like a free trade agreement can lead to vast rearrangements in societies in multiple countries at once. Whoever writes such an agreement has the chance to effectively direct those changes. Ringing the world with military bases (the US currently has upwards of 800) changes the playing field for those countries who may be staring down the barrel of a foreigner's gun. Powerful people can bring more things into existence than less powerful people can. Culture is made up of more of *their* things than those of the less powerful. Arrangements that entail conflicts of interest for public servants are smartly avoided in a fair society, yet such firewalls can be undone or outmaneuvered when there is the power to do so.

Many efforts to change the playing field aim at leveling it and are motivated by a desire to enhance the common good. For individuals who set out to help others—including nonhumans—it is important to notice that there would not be the positive feedback of augmented power that could otherwise give them an edge in the future. Influencing the world for self-gain feeds back while using power to help others generally does not.

3 Ethics and Winners

One candidate for the best single measure of the health of a society is whether ethical acts by someone lead them to do better or to do worse. It is the social and cultural environment we jointly create that determines this. If society is fair and the playing field is level, ethical acts will meet with rewards, while unethical behavior will be met with censure or setbacks of one sort or another. If society has tipped toward corruption, then the opposite will tend to be true.

While there are a number of important ways that a fair society can be self-reinforcing and stable, such a society will generally also remain vulnerable to infiltration by factions whose power and influence begins to grow and then to snowball. If there is a wedge by which this process can get started, it may be through advantages inherent in unethical behavior. A willingness to override moral constraints opens up an array of new options for an individual's personal gain. Unethical people have a large bag of tricks to draw from that ethical people do not have. Things one person will consent to that another will not include stealing, lying, bribing, despoiling the environment, or knowingly harming others. The widespread practice of externalizing costs also fits here. It is through alterations to the playing field that these practices can either become legal, or that a person can manage to escape notice or accountability. The more power such individuals have, the wider the scope of behaviors they can partake in or get away with.

Another way to look at this dichotomy between ethical and unethical behavior is that it is like two people playing the same game but with different rules. The ethical player is constrained by certain of their internal rules. When different rules are followed it is to be expected that the outcomes or "payoffs" will differ. Law enforcement, of course, when it is fairly administered, is supposed to make sure that unethical behavior does not net rewards.

The ethical component of our actions set precedents that influence the fabric of society. Today, corporate leaders, political candidates, investors, and most of the rest of us regularly face situations in which the more ethical choice is less beneficial, and the less ethical choice is more beneficial. When we choose the more, or the less, ethical, we set an example that may be emulated by others who witness our choice. We may also be sending a given message out into the marketplace, such as that we do or do not care about the ethics behind a product's manufacture. When individuals lie, they undermine the chance for honest people to be taken at their word. And if we are harmed or taken advantage of, it can subsequently affect our attitude and the way we treat and respond to others in turn. Likewise when we are treated respectfully. There are self-reinforcing paths in society that emanate from both ethical and unethical behaviors. As the boy who cried wolf learned from even his relatively innocent choice to fool his townsfolk, very real changes can result from disrupting subtle social constructs like trustworthiness. Simplistically stated, to a large extent good will breed more good, while bad will breed more bad.

Ethics and payoffs also apply to things as serious as fighting in war. Though it can seem incongruous to talk about rules in something as fundamentally unruly as war, there are, nonetheless, established guidelines for what is deemed acceptable or not. And these rules can and do get broken. A military that commits war crimes is engaged in a game in which, if they win the conflict, their crimes will be forgotten, and if they don't commit those crimes, they may lose. The applicable phrase "fighting dirty" even carries the connotation that that is how one would win. In general, if playing fair is going to win, it usually requires some form of referee—as with witnesses and accountability.

In a culture tipping toward corruption, one pattern that shows up has to do with the dynamics of temptation. It is realistic to imagine that a fraction of the population "has its price" for agreeing to join in on a given unethical practice. If the available payoff for that behavior rises as a result of a corrupted social setting, there will be more individuals for whom the price is enough, and who then will decide to participate, or, some would say, "sell out." Such temptations can be quite tangible as people get to witness a colleague making out like a bandit and know that they could as well.

In the above example, benefits or costs associated with the available choices shape society by bringing out different sides to the same person. If society rewards good behavior, that is what emerges, and we get more of it. When unethical behavior is what is rewarded, there is more of that in response. This means that the very same people act in different ways as the social context changes: each environment encouraging certain behaviors, while leaving others to go dormant. The promise implied by this perspective is that society would work beautifully if we could successfully create environments which brought out the best in people.

While registering and responding to incentives can bring out different sides to a person, it also may have the effect of moving people around, sorting them toward the niches that most reward them and that best match their aptitudes and their values. Both innate and acquired traits orient a person toward finding the positions in life that suit them the best. We all run a gauntlet in society, being screened for educational opportunities, employment, mates, and social circles. Some doors open, some do not. We like to excel at what we do, and our abilities and predilections guide us. We choose what we think will fulfill us, and others choose us for their reasons in turn. It is as if there were an invisible casting director sorting human beings into their most perfect roles. This is interesting in its own right because it is a part of the picture of how society acquires the characteristics that it does. But a sorting phenomenon also sheds light on a society's tendency toward corruption.

Humanity is so diverse that one can virtually assume the existence, somewhere, of any personality type. The interesting question then becomes, "where will these individuals each end up?" Will a modern-day Attila the Hun find a job, or will he have to sell pencils on the sidewalk because no one wants to hire him? Will a mean-spirited or ruthless or power-hungry person be marginalized by society, or will they discover that opportunities abound for them—and where would those specific niches be? In a corrupted society unethical people can become leaders of major corporations, hiring and firing to collect like-minded people under them. Sorting works by our moving both toward and away from things. When good people leave an agency or corporation of their own volition because of frustration over a clash of values, it further concentrates the subculture that they left behind. Skill sets that pair a flexible moral code with intellect or craftiness or charisma can be in high demand for the returns they bring to a business or venture. There may be selection by the "casting department" for people who, for instance, can lie straight-faced. If someone's job involves lying to the public or the press, and they do not do a convincing job, then they are replaced by someone who does it better—toward the point where the message is fully believed to be earnest and true.

Sorting fosters collaboration. As like-minded people find each other, self-reinforcing networks of individuals and institutions set up. Such a network could include lawmakers, regulators, think tanks, lobbyists, judges, and CEOs. This is cultural coevolution. Entities that have been in a longstanding association evolve together as a group and become dovetailed in their features and their interrelations.

A person opting out of a corrupted subculture may have the ethical choice of whether or not to become a whistleblower. The "climate" for whistleblowers at a given time in history varies and is itself revealing of the health of society. When this climate is poor, there are risks associated with speaking up, and there is a default reward for staying silent. With this silence is the inference that information is not being shared that would be in a more auspicious setting—in some cases things that could be significant to maintaining a vital democracy.

Ominously, with this collection of social system phenomena, a society could come to exist in which the least ethical people held the most power.

4 Persuasion and Manipulation

Human susceptibility to influence is a decisive factor in the shaping of society. Whatever the degree of our innate or immutable characteristics, nature has left an abundant amount of room for us to be molded by our surroundings—particularly by other humans. Information inputs, through social interaction, formal education, and exposure to media, build the individuals that we are, creating beliefs and value systems, and establishing preferences and desires that can last a lifetime. Information inputs also give us the daily grist that we process to make sense of our ever-changing world.

So who is in charge of all this input? Part of the answer is that it goes to the highest bidder. And there are plenty of bidders interested in this opportunity.

Persuasion as a concept is one end of a continuum, the other end of which would be called manipulation. Along this continuum there are enormous payoffs associated with being able to get others to act in the way one would like them to. We described power as a measure of a person's ability to influence the world around them. Influencing the behavior of other people is the most significant form that this takes. To successfully influence people is to get them to like you, love you, fear you, work for you, vote for you, buy your products, or even kill and die for you. It covers the spectrum of the primary arenas in society. To the extent to which power can be used to influence people, and influencing people can enhance the power of the influencer, then there is positive feedback in the dynamic, wherein power can lead to more power.

Any quest for substantive social change includes the need to wrest citizens' minds away from those who would control them for private gain. A battle is on for the sovereignty of our very identities—for our minds and psyches—and the elite in society appear to be highly motivated to control this ground.

Throughout history when people were being mistreated, they most likely knew it and only needed to hope for the right window of opportunity to then rebel and better their lot. Conceivably, society could face an unprecedented "sleepwalking" scenario in which the power of sophisticated persuasion obscured much of the reality of people's circumstances. An ability to shape the mind of another, even down to its inner recesses, is the most disquieting dimension of the full picture of how our society works, and is a feature that deserves to be carefully examined by citizens and academics alike.

5 Secrecy and Dissembling

Wherever there are potential gains to be made by individuals in society, there are the equivalent of incentives. The realm of secrecy and stealth is associated with many kinds of gain or advantage, and we find the behaviors to match.

The most innocent instances of secrecy are for good, as when we decide not to share important, but possibly troubling, things with our children, our parents, friends, and such. In society at large, governments will do the same, withholding information from the public in order to encourage confidence or to maintain order. Well-meaning officials and politicians are in a bind, deciding what is proper to share. They can't share anything that the nation's enemies could take advantage of. Regarding the economy, they can't share anything that could rattle the markets. They can't verbalize the strategic thinking that is an inescapable dimension of political life. In general, reasoning within the halls of power is so complex it is almost inevitable that a simplified, and possibly pacifying, version of events is what is presented to the public, often in close confidence and collaboration with prominent media outlets.

Even this best-case scenario presents some problems. As with keeping double books, once a parallel story begins, that track is driven more by the need to maintain consistency with itself than by allegiance to the real facts. A bifurcation sets up that has a life of its own, and is hard to undo or resolve. Reversing course on a half-truth or a lie is quite awkward; in addition to disclosing the initial bad news, it can be hard to fess up because it then includes the revelation that information was intentionally withheld in the first place. Public cultures of half-truths become established in this way.

Similarly, lying or concealing may initiate a positive feedback loop wherein the more someone lies, the more they need to, so that no peripheral information ends up hinting at the truth of a matter. Secrecy can thus breed more secrecy.

For both innocent and not-so-innocent reasons, governments effectively erect a wall behind which the public cannot see. In a contentious world this is partly for the broad purpose of national security, which includes military considerations. This creates a tier of overseers who are in the know, arguably a dangerous precedent in a democracy. Strategically, the military or an intelligence agency may disseminate a false story for foreign consumption. But to tell their own citizens the real story would undermine the ploy. So the home-country population is, at best, required to read between the lines, and at worst accepts, unquestioning, what can become an extended contrived reality. The group identity we call "nationalism" will allow national security secrets for the good of the country. But once a black box secret category gets established, it becomes a magnet and a temptation for individuals who have things to hide. "National security" can be used for cover for activities the public would not allow.

We mentioned that the reality of high-level reasoning and deliberation may be far too complex to share with the public. But we can guess that in a corrupted society, it is also too self-serving to share. In our personal lives there are checks on dishonesty, and major incentives for honesty. In public life, forthrightness depends crucially on mechanisms of accountability, such as an independent media and intact regulatory or oversight functions. Wealth and power enable the management or manipulation of information and the ability to thwart accountability. Succeeding at keeping meetings, agreements, programs, and budgets secret can give one an edge in acquiring or maintaining power and wealth. Because of incentives for not getting caught engaging in criminal or unethical activity, we can expect methods of secrecy and stealth to be sophisticated. The cultural selection pressure for this would be strong.

Secrecy includes some curious logic. It is a factor or feature that can enhance the perpetuation of something by evading the scrutiny that could curtail it. Because it is true, by definition, that secrets are not meant to be known, then there is an intrinsic problem in trying to evaluate them. What if there were a profoundly important secret that was also very well kept? How much could we learn about it? Who would advocate for its disclosure? What would their rationale even be, without knowing something about what the secret was? How can a person prove that something secret is secret? How can someone prove that there are not secrets?

Secrets related to public matters that are not carefully kept will succumb to probing journalists or investigators. So that would leave only the most cleverly-concealed secrets as the ones that survive—perhaps having never even been suspected. If someone were fully successful at maintaining a secret, then indeed, there would not be evidence to find. Of course, if something *truly* isn't there, then you will also not see it. So, exactly when and where we should try to see that which isn't easily seeable is a very real question. Potentially valuable critics of government or elite secrecy are in a catch-22, where the public will not engage a serious discussion about something with only marginal or incomplete evidence.

Corruption depends on secrecy. Rather than assume that corruption will be visible—and argue, for instance, that if something is not reported in *The New York Times*, then it must not be true—one should *expect* corruption to be underreported and hard to spot. The sheer complexity and inscrutability of certain crimes, including white collar crimes, are also factors in successful stealth. When lies or crimes go unexposed, it is a sign to certain others that "the coast is clear" to follow that lead.

It can be argued that the essence of what the US is about as a world power is the brilliant strategic success of saying it is great and good, while being bad. Think about it: saying it is good and *being* good is not likely to have been a winning formula for becoming a major power—at least in the past. Being bad (i.e. self-serving) and being honest about it is also not a winning formula for obvious reasons. Our remaining choice—for powerful elites to be self-serving and be dishonest about it—has many things going for it that would enable it to both take hold and then remain as the norm. This predicted state closely matches what we appear to have today. The US talks a blue streak about democracy and freedom, but its foreign policy over many decades has worked to thwart political and economic equality in all corners of the globe. The reason for the policy is simple: promoting real democracy means assenting to increase the power of others relative to oneself. The reason for the dishonesty is also simple: painting a rosy picture of one's motives fools enough people that it enables the practices to survive. By this measure the US, on the world scene, is the proverbial wolf in sheep's clothing.

There is a singularly clever ruse that has been noted publicly by the likes of both J. Edgar Hoover and Adolph Hitler. This is the logic of what is referred to as the big lie, the essence of which is that the more audacious a crime, the less it will be suspected or believed. People attempting to expose such a crime are pushed to the realm of claiming the preposterous, which, among other things, sharply raises their burden of proof. Counterintuitively, a lesser lie or crime may be harder to get away with than a greater lie or crime.

Included with the logic of deception has to be, ironically, the logic of self-deception. I say "ironically" because it is usually assumed that to deceive is to have ill motives and a certain calculation behind one's actions. But if an individual truly does not register their own artifice, they could feel entirely innocent, and win trust by projecting that innocence. This idea is elaborated in book length in *The Folly of Fools: The Logic of Deceit and Self-Deception in Human Life* by anthropologist Robert Trivers. The powerful underlying idea is that natural selection would have favored, and selected for, a self-unaware cheater over a self-aware cheater, resulting in a human trait that factors into the reasoning of social systems to this day. If there is good news, it is that natural selection would have also given us the skills to detect such a performance and avoid being cheated.

Nothing more directly accounts for the existence and survival of something in culture than that it cannot be seen or identified in order to be scrutinized and screened for its worth by broader society. Effective stealth enables many things to survive that would not survive if they saw the light of day.

6 Cooperation

Cooperation is often exclaimed to be the thing that, if only we did more of it, we would be a happier human family. This use of the word "cooperation" references the spirit of generosity or the virtue of flexibility, and also imagines that doing things jointly binds us together. All good here! We, though, will use a more circumscribed meaning for cooperation—something closer to "collaboration."

Humans generally have a keen sense for when something works in their favor or when it does not, and they will readily cooperate with others when the underlying arithmetic is right. People will cooperate, or collaborate, when they can do better together than they can alone.

Game theory modeling has revealed fascinating details of how and when cooperation is favored. The iterated prisoner's dilemma is one such edifying mathematical game, and several of its take-home lessons are as follows:

- Human psychology is such that we feel out each other's willingness to forgo private short-term gain in order to team up for greater long-term gain. If we get the right signals, we proceed, cautiously at first, into an ongoing reciprocal exchange. (One of the key forms of cooperation that is found in nature is called reciprocal altruism. This cooperation in nature follows essentially the same reasoning as that which has been elaborated for humans.)

- Cooperation needs a jumpstart. A generous offer or gesture serves as an invitation and a demonstration of good faith. A tendency to respond in turn usually starts the reciprocal exchange. More substantial indications of willingness to play can be offered if needed.

• Some leniency is a plus. This can prevent a closing down of "negotiations" before even getting off the ground. A lack of flexibility can end up leading to a string of retributions—to reciprocal punitive actions. Forgiveness, or its equivalent, can break such a chain or prevent it from happening in the first place.

• Toleration of cheating or of reneging can invite more of the same—so vigilance, plus some form of response or reprisal, is needed to maintain cooperation that has been established.

• If no end to the cooperation is anticipated, reciprocity may continue unchanged. If and when an end approaches, the logic of cooperation can abruptly shift and break down.

Some of these lessons are obvious, while others are not. If one has a goal of succeeding at cooperation, then book learning (of all things!) may be able to provide some surprise pointers.

People's receptivity to cooperation is related to how much power they have. Cooperation, like compromise, is motivated by seeking a potential better outcome. Intuitively, we can see that a person who has abundant power may not need to cooperate or compromise. The other party has to have something you need or want in order for it to be worth your while to engage with them in a reciprocal arrangement. As with comparative advantage in economics, or the division of labor in a partnership, an interdependence—i.e. a *lack* of independence—can be a good thing that fosters cooperation.

With no party too powerful, interdependence may be universally good. But when one party has greater power, the other can be highly vulnerable. If, for example, an effective monopoly is held on something essential for life, then it can be used for manipulation or extortion. If you are dependent, you will cooperate to maintain access to what you need—even with poor terms. If you are independent, you call the tune. There is an important power and freedom in self-reliance, though it is not as efficient as specialization with exchange.

Building reciprocal relationships can be, for individuals, like putting money in the bank in a parallel, non-monetary economy—creating "social capital." Interdependence and an ongoing connection means that you will help others, and be helped, yourself, in turn.

In relatively equal exchanges, there are numerous ways to foster cooperation. Negotiators and facilitators are specialists at this. But games modeled with equal players (such as the prisoner's dilemma) have only limited application for world problems that involve inequality.

As mentioned above, anything that reduces the expectation of long-term association will lead to less cooperation. The poet Gary Snyder once said that the most radical thing you can do is to stay in one place—by which he meant to live, and continue to live, in one community. A world characterized by transience is one that is a sitting duck for opportunism. Transience often means no accountability and no potential—thus no incentive—for building trust and building reciprocal relationships. In nature, long-term coexistence leads to coevolution of organisms and to dazzling examples of adaptations involving interdependence. Humans in stable societies throughout the world have their own cultural counterparts to this phenomenon.

If interacting is a one-shot deal, models say that people should exploit, if for no other reason than to avoid being exploited themselves. If a cooperative relationship is started, then defecting becomes more likely when a parting of the ways is in sight—again, something associated with transient social patterns. With certain long-term projects, payoffs can be concentrated at the end, just when relationships may be terminating. Numerous bank robbery movies, for instance, include a betrayal as the need for a team effort falls away!

Curiously, there may be dynamics similar to this that are afoot among certain elites. Whether their purported plans for world domination are working on schedule, or not working well at all, there may be moments when defecting for a cash-in or to act on a personal obsession or vendetta becomes too great a temptation. Some individuals may want to break ranks to hasten a plan because they are growing old or are otherwise impatient to see it fulfilled, conceivably leading to a false step. Defecting for a plea bargain is another scenario if and when an elite crime is on the verge of exposure.

A key rationale that may be leading the world toward oblivion involves not wanting to unilaterally scale back such that others would gain ground in relation to you. The alternative—agreeing in a negotiation with another to both "do without" so that parity is maintained—is a significant and familiar form of cooperation. This can enable a mutual goal that neither would attempt alone because of the disadvantage they would sustain. Cuts in greenhouse gas emissions, nuclear weapons reductions, fishing catch limits, and a truce in war are examples. This follows our condition for cooperation: in the big picture, doing better jointly than apart—collaborating toward this end, instead of competing and suffering its associated costs.

7 Technology

Many things about society are mutable, or ebb and flow with the passage of time. A few processes, however, are both inexorable and irreversible. The progression of technology is just such a one-way affair. In addition to a never-ceasing introduction of new capabilities into our cultural landscape, there is a ratcheting effect in which whatever is discovered cannot then be undone.

Aptitude for inventing—and with it the corresponding motivation to invent—is part of our genetic inheritance, having increased our biological fitness. In organized culture we face a raft of incentives for inventing and for pursuing technological innovation—factors that have been a constant driving force for the changes that marked civilization from its start. We are enamored of the capabilities technology can provide. The human—and particularly the young male—fascination with superheroes speaks to a deep attraction in us for capacities that give us advantage. At any one cultural moment, the next innovation—be it fire, flight, or Wi-Fi—can seem as magic, with us the magicians.

Nearly every imagined new technology represents a temptation to somebody. Thus the most obvious aspect of technological life that appears to be inescapable is if something *can* be done, then it most likely *will* be done. Whether laser beams from space, self-driving cars, mini-bots to do our housecleaning, or the engineering of new life forms, if it can be figured out, it is almost impossible to stop. Many technologies have little or no negative consequence, but others pose threats both known and unknown, including ones with gargantuan implications. It is disconcerting to think the path of civilization is tethered to such an absurdly simple notion: that technology cannot be resisted. The reasoning that accounts for this apparent inevitability includes the following:

- If I don't do it, someone else will—so my not doing it won't prevent it from happening.

- Even though someone else will eventually do it, I can gain at least a temporary, and perhaps decisive, advantage if I do it first.

- If it is a morally questionable technology, the moral person is at a loss knowing that a less moral person would seize the chance without hesitation, and perhaps use it to the detriment of others.

- Sometimes a technology needs to be developed to use as a bargaining chip against an adversary or competitor.

- If money can be made developing a technology, then incentive exists to develop it.

These rationales and motives lead people toward the choice to pursue technological innovation and to push at its cutting edge. Laws and public opinion can provide constraints or disincentives in some situations, but may just drive the development underground. Because of the cost of most advanced technologies, it is the elite who will have first choice in developing and dominating ones that they decide are of use to them. The added capability of new technologies means there is more power in their hands. Among the presumptive adversaries the elite have are the people from whom they steal resources, money, and liberties. Technologies that are applicable to defending elite privilege against the masses, domestically or overseas, would certainly be sought.

Elites may be empowered and emboldened by technologies that increase their advantage. Having the capability to immobilize an angry mob at the push of a button makes it more likely that they would make choices that arouse an angry mob in the first place. The threat of aroused ire is lower when such technology is yours to use.

The advantage one has from a new technology is often enhanced if the research and development, and in some cases the product itself, can be kept secret. The potential gains from keeping powerful technologies secret is one reason to believe there is probably much that is currently not known to the world public. Again, technological or war-fighting capabilities that depend on secrecy for effectiveness against an enemy will be unknown to the citizenry of the home country as well.

The largest technological gambles that humans are engaged in are said to go by the initials GNR, for genetic engineering, nanotechnology, and robotics. Creations that replicate themselves on their own or have intelligence that escapes human management are among the things to picture here. Certain emerging technologies are likely to be game changers, and these will probably include advances in the psychological programming of humans. The implications for manipulating a live human to carry out commands is staggering, and for this very reason has most certainly been actively pursued by factions somewhere. The greater the payoff, the keener the pursuit, the more likely the actualization.

Social inventions like banking and financial practices can be thought of as technologies as well. One arrangement that has been cited as a factor in political tectonics in at least the last several centuries is the fact of governments borrowing the money they need at interest. If private citizens could interpose themselves in this process, then not only would there be profit to be made on the volume, but there would also be people with an incentive to lobby or manipulate a government to spend more. Influence over the money supply itself would offer further advantages. Countries, including the US, have at various times used other systems for public financing. The historic determination of powerful individuals to implement private central banks, by hook or by crook, is a clue that something may be rotten in Denmark.

The range of strategic methods for gaining and holding on to power can be likened to a technology or a science, and, presumably, continually advances in sophistication. We have every reason to believe that this specialization is a product of progressive trial and error and of accumulated mastery on a par with human achievement in other realms.

The race for advantage in competitive markets—like that between superpowers—is an "arms race" where catching up, then inching ahead, becomes the cyclical and relentless imperative. Ever-advancing technologies exemplify this dynamic. There is no standing still. This is the same logic that drives natural selection: genes for *not* trying to advance soon seal an organism's fate as a "has been." It is a puzzle, in society, to figure out how to extract ourselves from this kind of cycle. *If* technological advances could magically stop, everyone would catch up and thereafter have parity—which would provide a better basis for negotiating peace or cooperation. The mindset of anticipating the next technological advantage one could gain poisons the well of possibilities for the human actors who are locked into this game.

Once, as Jared Diamond masterfully lays out in his book *Guns, Germs, and Steel: The Fates of Human Societies*, differences such as that between bronze versus steel weaponry were decisive in directing the course of large swaths of history. Multiple, extremely sophisticated technological frontiers could be decisive today, many having to do with the largely invisible realm of electronics and computer programs. Brain power is perhaps the most important element in this unnerving, fast-changing game. Today, a teenage hacker from their bedroom in Kolkata could be the wild card that brought whole nations to heel.

A simple cost-benefit model tells us that something will be undertaken if the benefits of it outweigh the costs. But if the benefits of a given choice are very high, that may encourage someone to tolerate, rationalize, or justify dangerous associated costs that may also be high. Technologies are notorious for tempting fate in this way. This is the case, for example, with depleted uranium weaponry. Its advantages in war fighting are so significant that the danger of radioactive poisoning is downplayed. In this example, if the costs were accrued directly to the decision-makers, the arithmetic would certainly change. In other cases a risk is willingly taken on, based on the advantage. The concept of large benefits motivating the acceptance of potential or actual costs is a universal one, and applies to a range of human endeavors, including the pleasure of recreational activities such as race car driving, extreme skiing, or the use of certain drugs. It also could account for why some marriages are rocky, a specific temptation having overridden an incompatibility.

An objective accounting of risks will not be forthcoming in a corrupted society. If we do not have quality science that is safely insulated from the profit motive, we cannot even trust facts and will be unable to make prudent and measured decisions as a populace about potential threats from both existing and emerging technologies.

8 Psychology and Circumstance

There are two halves to the process of evolution in culture—a back and a forth. First, humans change things in the cultural environment by their political, economic, and interpersonal behavior. Second, our psychology interprets and assesses the new environment to then guide our political, economic, and interpersonal behavior in response. Actions result in changes, which dictate new and different actions—and around it goes. How we choose to engage the cultural environment determines its evolution.

As a sideline to our discussion, we have been speculating on whether or not elite behavior is responsible for most of the world's problems. The elite have the most power and wealth and frequently act for their self-gain at the expense of much else. But is it not inevitable that most people will base their actions on a cost-benefit assessment of the choices available to them? Like water flows downhill, people will spot opportunities to gain and choose them over not gaining. So how could we reasonably expect the elite to do otherwise?

It is always a good exercise to try to put oneself in another's shoes. In the case of the elite, they are what they are largely because they play a no-holds-barred game in society. When the mindset of an individual is competitive, and they seek to be on the cutting edge, they are subject to a cruel logic. As mentioned in the context of an arms race when talking about technology, if people don't take every chance to move forward, they move backward by default, relative to others. And it is true—true in culture, just as it is in nature. A precept of this book is that, for culture, we solve this troublesome reality by changing the environment in which the elite (and all of us) act. So, in theory, the elite (to the extent to which they are still elite) continue to act for their own best interest, but, having now changed the costs and the benefits of many things in society, their choices would be compatible with the common good. Their best choice for moving forward, in other words, is now not a threat, and no dilemma of society somehow needing its members to use self-restraint, remains.

Action/non-action

One of the confounding things about the tendency of a democracy to drift, when it does, toward inequality, is that it could be easily prevented. The drift involves a shifting of power and wealth from one group to another. Before this imbalance becomes advanced, there is plenty of leverage available to correct the drift. But, ironically, there is usually little appreciation of the need, and little motivation to act, until signs of disenfranchisement are obvious.

If this drift is checked in time, society can settle into a stabilizing, negative feedback pattern, such as the following: When wealth is shared and times are good, people are comfortable and less inclined to be engaged in the politics around them. If inequality grows, both displeasure and awareness increase, and people become politically active. Change is effected, and as equality returns, comfort and passivity return together, and the cycle repeats.

But, for at least one reason, this cycle may not necessarily repeat. Since the very ability to restore equality wanes as power concentrates, there is clearly a point at which it is too late, and the more powerful members of society have the power to keep things that way. This is the conundrum we speculated on at the beginning of this chapter.

One version of the negative feedback pattern is the case of revolution, instead of timely reform, as the response to power concentration: Victorious from ousting an abusive elite, people create the best new society they can. This subsequently degenerates over time from greed coupled with myriad positive feedback loops, until social conditions become intolerable. The elite of that society are then overthrown, and the revolution creates the best society that it can going forward.

An intended distinction here is that, in the first scenario, the swing between corruption and reform is not dramatic, and the drift toward power concentration is caught early. In the revolution example, we can imagine a great abuse of power, and a great subsequent suffering of, and anger within, the population. But in both cases the conundrum is solved because the motivation and savvy of the public is adequate to restore a balance and a relative equality to society. There is minor power concentration in one case, and a major concentration in the other. Whether or not the power associated with rising discontent can or cannot check elite power accumulation is a key question, and one that we will return to.

Patterns of waxing and waning activism show other variations. If a natural resource like an old growth forest is in good condition, people may feel that it can safely sustain some impact—cutting, in this case. After a degree of deterioration, the integrity of the resource is in question, and its preservation becomes the center of concern and activism. However, beyond a point of decline, the case for preservation weakens, and interest and activism fade. The more that is lost, the less people have a viable asset to advocate for. This fact is used strategically by certain industries who expedite destructive effects so opposition will find itself *beyond* the point of the strongest case and the greatest motivation. Change which is slow has a different kind of problem in that it can be hard to detect for its very slowness, limiting our response as a consequence. We can easily lose perspective on the quality of such things as consumer goods, nature, or our standard of living, when change is incremental.

Progressive organizations, including alternative media, are subject to several subverting temptations that shape their actions. By softening their message, they may obtain more funding, enjoy the gratifying feeling of having a wider audience, and avoid harassment by those who would object to the advancement of more incisive or controversial perspectives. Strategic though this may be, these factors can also inch a counterforce closer to being a neutral or neutered force.

If living conditions in society were to deteriorate significantly for any reason, then there would be consequent changes in our behavior. A breakdown of supply lines or infrastructure, for example, could bring out the best in people as they rally to help each other out. But scarcity and adversity can also bring out some of the worst, with an every-person-for-themselves mindset. Like a run on a bank, or on comestibles at the supermarket during a truckers' strike, positive feedbacks kick in that can quickly exacerbate a situation.

There may be a large segment of the population that tend to be followers who will go along with whatever the primary currents are in society. Through positive feedback, this faction would augment whatever course society takes—not unlike a rowboat half full of water, where each direction the occupant leans, the water follows.

If motivation to challenge abuse of concentrated power does materialize, that threat can activate elite motivation in reaction. In proportion, the more effective the populace is in its efforts, the stronger could be the response.

As a society becomes corrupted, there can be a growing risk associated with speaking one's beliefs. With more people being mum— or acting falsely on purpose—it is harder to know what the balance of power actually is. This adds a dynamic element to culture. Individuals could make false moves by misjudging others. Since people would mostly be muting their opposition to powerful interests, it might be hard to know when and if society were close to a critical mass of resistance, and there could be surprises.

Investment

One meaning for the word "investment" is "progress down a path along which costs are accrued that would have to be repeated in one form or another along other, alternative, paths." Momentum builds up along the paths we invest in, as, for example, with a career or with the chosen route to a destination. This makes it easier to keep going in the same direction than to change directions. When we invest time, effort, or resources in something—and thus have a stake in it—our behavior will reflect this. Certain human problems have to do with the logic of this momentum. The monumental scale of society's investment in the use of fossil fuels comes to mind. In the US we chose not to adopt the metric system because we had invested in the system that we had and did not want to start over. Our chosen system of measure may or may not be a problem today, but short-term reasoning can consign us to inefficient ways of doing things. Long-term thinking that includes the option to begin anew can have large benefits. Our judgment can also suffer when we have made a major investment in something. If you were 500 feet from the summit of a mountain after a month of effort, and a serious storm closed in, would you make as safe a choice as you would on a lesser peak? We have each invested in our path in life, too. Our identity itself can be looked at as a set of criteria around which we make an investment. In life we like to do what we are good at and have worked to be good at. If we have studied war, or have studied peace, we will have a bias toward that which we know. When it comes to changing course for a longer-term benefit, larger egos make it harder to change, smaller ones make it easier.

People have speculated that our permanent war economy in the US originated because of temptations from the investment associated with tooling up for WWII. It is a reasonable idea. In theory, one war could tip incentives toward more war.

Elite mindset

The idea that an unequal distribution of wealth and power may be almost a law of nature is not lost on the elite subculture, many of whom understand it and its implications. A belief that inequality will be a given and some form of a ruling class is inevitable in society leads some to reason that it is right to take part in creating that outcome. It also simply presents the choice of being a future "have" or future "have not." Factored into this logic is the familiar rationalization that "if I don't do it, someone else will," or its close cousin, "if they are doing it, I will (need to) too." These temptations apply to many small and large choices and clearly may get worse when there are unprincipled actors in the game setting their ante. Elites may be operating with the idea that democracy can't and won't prevail, and therefore the battle is over who will be on top in the future unequal social order.

Carte blanche power may foster progressively weirder thinking, desires, and goals that can lead individuals to push or break the bounds of normal social behavior. When there is no reason to have to compromise or to please others, then what happens? Excess power may be a sort of poison, and civilized behavior will be the norm only when no one has access to such power. Fascinating recent experiments by Paul Piff of the University of California, Irvine—in addition to well-known early work on this subject (e.g. the Stanford prison experiment)—bear out the observation that power subverts respectful behavior. Environment and our circumstances bring out the better or the not-so-better sides of who we are.

Ironically, socially detrimental actions of elites and others may be motivated by a sense of trying to avoid being the loser in one's peer group, rather than necessarily needing to be a winner. Status and achievement are relative—including in the billion-dollar-a-year bracket.

9 Accountability

A natural tendency for humans to track and evaluate each other's behavior leads to the notion of accountability and an attention to who should or should not be answerable for which actions and consequences.

Who's responsible?

Though social mores exist that say we should be accountable for the actions we undertake, it is surprisingly unclear how to apply this in practice. Herein lies an important explanation for a wide range of human troubles. Who is actually responsible—and therefore should be accountable—for what, in a long train of interconnected events? Where, in different instances, should responsibility ultimately, or primarily, lie? These questions get played out in six verses of the Bob Dylan song "Who Killed Davey Moore?," in which everyone from the boxing match fans to the dead boxer's opponent get to answer "not I" to the title's question. "Who drove the passenger pigeon to extinction?" or "who created the (still healing) ozone hole?" are questions that would tend to get the same answer. Who all but eliminated the thousand-year-old forests of the Pacific Northwest? The consumer of the wood products? The logging industry entrepreneurs? The person wielding the chainsaw?

This puzzle is compounded when you factor in persuasion, indoctrination, and other forms of social conditioning. To mark one end of a spectrum, if a person commits a crime under the influence of a hypnotist, who is responsible for that crime? Most people would say "the hypnotist." More realistically, if a person watches TV all day and votes for politicians who launch immoral wars, then who is most responsible for those wars? If that same person read *The New York Times* and *The Wall Street Journal* instead, what then? Would they be more, or would they be less, responsible? The people who write or produce the news mostly have no malice. But they are at the helm of a powerfully influential medium and may be perpetuating beliefs or ideas that cause harm. It would seem obvious enough that individuals who choose to smoke cigarettes, or who attempt to live off of junk food, are the ones most responsible for any health consequences they'd sustain. But if the product makers utilize cutting-edge advertising techniques to market these items, how much is the individual properly to blame? Effective manipulation, after all, causes people to act out the wishes of the manipulator.

As a general question, how responsible can you expect a citizen to be if they are subjected to calculated persuasion? Finding ways to recognize who rightly bears responsibility, and thus should be accountable, for which actions—including within the context of intentional manipulation—is an important subject for society to sort out. Potential criteria for accountability could involve how much a person knows, how much they "should" know, how much power they have, or how directly or closely linked their actions are to a consequence. One well-known precedent for responsibility, set by the Nuremberg Trials after World War II, is that following orders is not an excuse when committing immoral acts. But, in at least the military application of this rule, how can a soldier who has been fed a soup-to-nuts diet of "America, land of the free and home of the brave" be expected to discern what orders to obey or disobey?

Remoteness of cause and effect

The remoteness of cause and effect is another factor that confounds the accountability process. If a health problem in newborn babies is being caused by endocrine-disrupting effects of a chemical that was activated by sunlight after leaching out of plastic consumer goods in a landfill that has been closed for twenty years, who should or could be accountable for the health problem? Over 500 aboveground nuclear tests between 1945 and 1980 may have been responsible for millions of premature deaths worldwide. But would it even be possible to establish cause and effect over the entire globe during an approximately seventy-five-year span? When an action and its consequence are remote in either space or time, it is often difficult to recognize or demonstrate the connection between the two.

Long and not-so-obvious chains of causation throw us off the scent of what effects come from which of our actions. Did US foreign policy help to lower the cost of labor overseas (by creating poverty and therefore a powerless work force in many countries) and contribute to jobs offshoring? Was it partly a desire for cheaper consumer goods that drove "Made in the USA" businesses out of business? Was there a positive feedback loop in which the more that jobs left the US, the more the then financially-strapped Americans created demand for inexpensive goods, the more their jobs left?

When stolen things change hands, the potential to trace or enforce accountability is largely broken. This could be true of a watch or a bicycle, but is also true of such things as the Louisiana Purchase. Elaborate financial derivatives breed on the cover that this same kind of multiparty remoteness provides. So-called "plausible deniability" is an invention that achieves a similar result, enabling a plea of innocence.

Corporate structure/ singular acts

Institutional structures sometimes make responsibility disappear altogether. Corporate board members believe they are in service to shareholders; CEOs are paid to do a job; shareholders watch stock performance, not business practices; consumers are remote from, or under-informed about, the details of the manufacture of a product; politicians and regulators are ingratiated to a confusing array of constituents and are disproportionately influenced by the most influential. No one currently fully shoulders the ethical ramifications of a corporation's behavior. This fact of missing, diluted, or dispersed accountability is the essential explanation for why detrimental business practices survive as they do.

If the search for where "the buck stops" defies easy accounting, then more elusive still is grasping the arithmetic behind cumulative effects. Many large and important outcomes in society originate with the singular acts of individuals. If it takes the ecological footprints of a billion people to begin to adversely impact the seas or the atmosphere, it is easy to think that being one one-billionth of a problem is almost equal to nothing. From there it is also easy to suppose that it does not really matter how we alone act. The same reasoning can be applied to voting, purchasing habits, or touching a sculpture that says "Do not touch." It is helpful to our perspective when we witness an example like an election that is won by just a handful of votes. It is also helpful to have intermediate examples of our impacts, both bad and good, to bridge the conceptual gap—things like the human imprint on a neighborhood park or a successful "buy local" campaign. Sometimes our actions are less singular than we think. Depending on how we are regarded in our social networks, the ways that we act and even our guiding values and philosophies may be copied or adopted by others.

Countering accountability/externalities

All of this said, however, the primary cause of the breakdown of accountability in society is intentional efforts to impede it. A system that enforced accountability would be unfavorable for players who gain from being unaccountable. When those individuals have the power to do so, they change the system to work in their favor. Complex legal instruments and disclaimers are created to insulate corporations from criminal liability for almost anything their companies might engage in. Infiltration of regulatory agencies and lobbyists that influence laws bearing on accountability cover additional bases. Penalties for broken laws, when they are less than the profits made by the offending activity, fail to serve as disincentives. Companies owned by companies owned by companies—creating "anonymous companies"—and registered offshore in "secrecy jurisdictions," is an obfuscation trick that enables people to escape accountability, including dodging taxation. Presidential pardons and various immunities shield yet more players. The information output of the media and of academia do not give the public all that it requires in order to play its primary role as advocates for responsible behavior. The United States is able to ignore or break treaties, and often be unaccountable on the world stage, because of its brute strength alone. A social environment that fails to create accountability is, to a large degree, a product or outcome of efforts by powerful people to achieve just that.

In the marketplace, one constructive vision for accountability is embodied by the idea of full-cost accounting. Numerous commercial activities currently place burdens on members of the public, other organisms, or on the commonly held resources of society. These negative externalities reflect costs that have been avoided by producers and are not represented in the price of their goods. Full-cost accounting would mean one of two things: that the externalized costs were calculated and added to the price of the good as, for example, a tax or tariff; or, that there were no externalities, and the product was created and priced accordingly. In either case the higher accurate price of the product would lead naturally to corrections in the market, to leveling the playing field between competing goods, and to the reinforcing of honorable business practices. The "accounting" of accountability is answered here by the honest pricing.

10 Asymmetries

One of the dynamics we are focusing on is the conflicting interests between a small, wealthy subculture we have been calling the "elite," and the balance of a population. "Class conflict" is the familiar term for this. Thinking in categories usually involves oversimplifications, but there are useful insights to extract from this way of picturing society. These two groups differ from each other in size, power-per-person, and to some extent intent, leading to striking differences in relevant strategy and behavior.

The elite generally have to keep their plans concealed. They hide their motives and goals and, when needed, they hide the true nature of their deeds. By contrast, the objectives of the populace-opposition can be announced and promoted. Generally, there are no malevolent acts by this opposition. While the elite are seeking or creating inequality, much of the populace is seeking the fairness of equality.

Elite strategies can be conceived by small groups of individuals and implemented via hierarchical organizations they have helped shape. An elaborate plan can be figured out and carried out. The populace-opposition has to disseminate its plans in public, in part because the power of this group relies on a large number of adherents. Secret plans, with their strategic advantages, would be limited to populace groups with few participants. Complex plans are harder to implement en masse, and any plan that could be foiled because of elite knowledge of it may need to be ruled out. Historically, opponents of repressive governments have devised ways to communicate with each other to skirt some of these obstacles.

In this age of surveillance, the elite increasingly have an ability to spy on and monitor the citizenry. Public access to government information, on the other hand, is on the decline (barring occasional leaks for which whistleblowers may pay a high price), and virtually nothing from the elite inner sanctums is accessible. This dichotomy translates into more power for the elite and less for the general public.

The populace has the opportunity to make change by example, highlighting a successful alternative version of a business, farming method, banking model, or governing structure. The elite generally do not benefit from showcasing their examples. Stealth is needed to prevent the detection of certain elite actions. Slow-and-steady is one stalking strategy that is found in nature. Short bursts followed by stasis is another. There are counterparts to both of these in society today, when and where elites attempt to obscure encroachments on the welfare of the public.

The cumbersome nature of democracy and inclusiveness is itself a structural thing that may slow down decision-making, organizing, and action. This fact can contribute to shaping society at large, since efficient, hierarchical decision-making may simply get more done, expediting the plans of those who use that modality. A process that is virtuous but slow may at times lose out to one that is less democratic but expedient. Hierarchies can also unselfconsciously replicate themselves, as the people for whom it was a successful method choose to use it again.

Hierarchy is not synonymous with autocratic decision-making, since in the best cases it needs cooperation and approval to be upheld and maintained. A hierarchy put in place for its efficiency can just as easily be dismantled if it fails to serve its purpose. Nevertheless, where there are hierarchical structures, there is greater reason for scrutiny and oversight. In some cases hierarchies are—like a pecking order—the product of bottom-up processes, rather than being the result of a plan. Sorting based on how much power each person has can lead to this social organization, with few having the most power and many having less.

Generally, it is highly motivated people who most shape the world. So who can we predict is likely to be the most motivated? It might be rare to find individuals with a strong motivation to create equal wealth distribution since monetary payoff is minor. It could be common, on the other hand, to find highly motivated individuals who want to make changes in government and society that favor themselves since the payoffs could be large. In addition, the more power one has, the more incentive there is to use it because of its greater ability to yield results. People with little power may have correspondingly less enthusiasm and less motivation to act to shape the world. The work of citizenship deters people when they can rationalize that their contribution is insignificant. This is one facet of the challenge of how to mobilize the participation needed to maintain democracy.

The oversimplification of using the term "populace" needs at least one qualification. What we are calling the "elite" is only those individuals who *succeeded* at becoming very powerful and does not include all of those who aspired to be. So it is really an open question what percentage of the population is or is not interested in an egalitarian society. Of those individuals with relatively little power, some want parity, but others surely would like to be a future Bill Gates.

Asymmetrical contests similar to those between the elite and the populace-opposition can be, and are, commonly explored in simulated game theory games. One case can be made, as an example, that in a population of selfless or merely innocent individuals, a selfish person will have a field day. Picture a town where no one locked their doors, or where people all took you on your word. Such populations could foster an increasing number of cheaters who took advantage of them. Similarly, picture a population of selfish individuals and ask "Would a selfless or naive person do well among them?" The answer could easily be "no." So where does a selfless person stand a chance? Back to the real world, if one group is known publicly to be pacifists, then is that not a temptation to some other group to conquer them? For a country to have no military may be the equivalent. So in an era of conquering, the only players left in the game are armed players, even if strictly for defense. These are puzzles that experts in key fields can help us solve.

Any time something goes in one direction more easily than it does in the other, there is the basis for a developing phenomenon or pattern. Land being divided into progressively smaller pieces or public ownership going toward private ownership are two examples. Cultures becoming homogenized through intermingling is another. In a similar vein it takes great labor, time, and skill to construct things, while the very same things can be destroyed in the blink of an eye. A million or more hours of human labor, for example, can be undone in a few minutes of a modern bombing campaign. Chaos and disorder are relatively easy to create—so easy, in fact, that it is smart to be sure people with that inclination do not have that chance.

It is also smart to have a ready awareness of which human actions can be reversed or undone if they do not work out and which cannot. If you dump confetti out of an airplane, what is done in a second would take years to only incompletely undo. Life has many examples more serious than this one that illustrate things we cannot undo and that bear on the course of civilization.

11 Enculturation

Paradoxically, there are problems associated with the fact that humans and their behavior are both mutable and immutable. Immutable represents the "nature" side of who we are; mutable the "nurture" side.

Society, at any given time, is populated by features that have prevailed, or come to exist, for some good reason. Often that reason is the capacity to win out via a contest. That contest could be for market share in an industry or between politicians in an election, but the ultimate of contests is that between whole nations or cultures. There is almost no corner of the globe today that does not have a history of conquest behind it. In the course of these conflicts any culture that was vanquished by another did not get to properly teach and socialize their next generation. The victors had that privilege. Vanquished cultures throughout history must certainly have included many highly worthy traits. That body of human cultural possibility has, in each era, and to different degrees, been lost to the world. The most obvious thing that a victor culture teaches is that it is virtuous, sometimes turning the meaning of the word utterly on its head in the process. The balance of what would be taught by the victor, and lost from a losing culture, would in each instance be a complex and interesting yarn to unravel. This selection process is significant and begs the question of what, indeed, those eclipsed cultures would be like if they had remained undisturbed.

And this process has not ceased to this day. Consider how much of the cultural heritage and the intact enculturation potential has been lost from the country of Iraq in recent decades, between the first Gulf War, crippling sanctions, and the decimation that ensued from March 2003. It may be a strategy of empires to specifically target an opponent's cultural foundations in order to undermine national and cultural identity and thus impact the capacity to resist. North Americans may themselves be a prime example of a people enculturated by the values associated with victors, in that we are historically blasé about brutal interventions elsewhere after being heirs to one of the largest conquests in history. With all of this said, long-standing cultural traditions *are* a powerful basis for the identity of a people and *do* survive to varying degrees in conquered lands.

The cultural and parental influences that have contributed to shaping well-rounded or moral or intellectually inquisitive people are usually quite apparent. The same is true for many character traits. It is rare, in my experience, to meet a person who does not show a congruence between upbringing, or cultural milieu, and adult character. This is one sign of the potential that nurture has in influencing who we become. A component of this package of influences in the developed world is the persistent, profit-driven persuasion of advertising, public relations, and political propaganda. People in the US have, as a result, been inculcated with beliefs that benefit the most powerful actors in society. We are not just the product of victors in geopolitics but are increasingly the product of victors in the marketplace and in the financial and power contests of our time. We are being socialized by Disney, Northrop Grumman, and Citibank as they infuse our culture with material that is consistent with their bottom line.

Layered atop this is the problem that *if* someone has been successfully indoctrinated, they would not be able to see that they have been—and probably would not appreciate being told so. This begins to resemble the puzzle of how to deprogram a brainwashed cult member. If reclaiming a democracy depends on a waking up, yet people don't believe that they are asleep in the first place, where does that leave us? This can be spoken of in degrees. If an activist is cognizant of only a portion of the corruption we face in the US, then how much of which problems can they solve?

The subject of enculturation has an added twist. Our individual beliefs, values, and attitudes are shaped, and shaped early, by cultural forces. Once ingrained, they are not easily changed. Culture, consequently, has inertia. As parents, we will teach what we know and not teach what we don't. We will model what we are and not something else. This inertia may mean that culture is not easily disrupted, but it also means that, once altered, it will not change easily from its new state. Presently, in what has arguably become a degraded cultural environment in the US—with people inured to accounts of torture and indefinite detention, accepting of encroachments on their liberties, and largely passive in the face of glaring corruption—we have a new question to consider: Is there now more inertia behind a corrupted culture than there is behind a fading one that we romanticize and may have taken for granted?

We began this chapter by framing the fact that a faltering democracy can come to face a conundrum: Once power slips from the hands of the citizenry, how does that citizenry have enough sway left to regain it? Here, discussing enculturation, we face a similar conundrum.

It takes wise people to make wise people, caring people to make caring people, and honest people to make honest people. What if it happened that enough wisdom, kindness, and integrity, or the wherewithal to feel righteous indignation, was culturally bred out of a people, so that there was no longer the capacity to instill those virtues in a new generation of children? And if liberties, for example, slip for a generation, would we lose sight of them or lose the expectation of having them? We may no longer demand things we were not taught are our birthright.

The demise of certain societies historically could, theoretically, have been related to a similar kind of enculturation bind. Taught and learned attributes of a culture can degrade in ways that impact the calculus of survival. Fidelity in the transmission of cultural material can be faulty or continuity broken altogether. To be not passed on once to a new generation is to have something be lost forever in that form. Maintenance of the quality of knowledge, know-how, and wisdom requires special attention to the transfer process, as with traditional guilds, systems of higher education, or the deliberate cultivation of morals.

There are many ways in which our fate could become sealed by the logic of our human circumstances. Like an air leak in a siphon, loss of continuity of civilized behavior is one of them. The capacity a culture has for maintaining itself, or changing its trajectory for the better, can be hobbled or even lost beyond a point of cultural breakdown. Though natural selection would have engineered a balance between nature and nurture in order to prevent culture (nurture) from lowering our fitness, culture is now a more formidable factor in shaping human behavior than it ever has been in our formative evolutionary past. Would our biological default settings enable us to push through complex cultural influences, overcome a potential "air leak," and come out unscathed? Or can the fact of cultural drift, and its subsequent propagation, lead us down a road we'd rather not be on? To the extent to which cultural transmission is ushering forward the "work" of many generations of great care and attention, we, today, are now its custodians and its lifeline.

CHAPTER THREE

Triangulating Where We Stand

One question that has been left in our laps by the preceding two chapters is "If positive feedback power accumulation is happening in US society, then what can or would stop it?" Any time there is positive feedback in a system, it is natural to ask, what happens next? If a quantity is growing over time and it cannot grow forever, then how, when, and why does the pattern change? With wealth and power in a human social system, the answers might include that checks and balances embedded in the laws of the land act to stabilize these variables or that citizen movements step in to do the same. Because of the obvious danger of power concentration growing to a point of tyranny, it behooves us to have a considered answer at hand for this important question.

As to whether or not—or to what extent—power concentration and its attendant corruption have been taking place in the US, this should be able to be answered through the output of scholars and journalists and be readily available to consider. But exactly *whose* accounting and *which* particular facts or documentation would we believe if sources turned out to differ? And if there is a trend in which democratic institutions are being corrupted, and wealth and power inequality is growing, is that something that would be easy for us to observe and identify on our own? The breadth and depth of our participation in society is largely shaped and guided by what we know and what we believe. Change what we believe, and you've changed our behavior; change the information we evaluate, and you likewise change our behavior. A personal aim of becoming informed as a citizen is not something that is at all straightforward or easy to achieve, and herein may lie one of the most complex obstacles to effective social change. Finding facts that are indeed facts, and analysis that is thorough and truly objective, takes a skill set and a diligence that is above average, to say the least. Against an array of factors and forces that complicate the effort, it is a significant challenge for citizens to learn enough to be astute and powerful political actors.

Shrewd citizenship

We can venture that many of the elite engage life—or at least business—as a kind of chess game at which they are very skilled. To the extent to which we share that same chessboard with them—the economy, the political sphere, etc.—we are in the same game and may be stuck needing to engage the elite in that arena. If we choose to pass or defer, we thereby forfeit, leaving others to win. To use another game analogy, if a whole sector of society that may include some of the wealthiest and most powerful individuals among us decides to play hardball, what choice does that give the rest of us? While *not* everyone's preferred style, adopting a version of a competitive spirit might be the difference between losing some very important things (like freedom, health, biological diversity, natural beauty, friendly international relations) or preserving and retaining those same assets. To be shrewd, the dictionary tells us, is to be astute or to have and show sharp powers of judgment. Being shrewd is winning, and embracing some form of it may stand the citizenry in good stead. A trained mind can learn to identify sophism and flawed reasoning or better judge the character of a public figure. Literacy in science and history give us the ability to understand complex issues or to respond with authority in public discussions. And since when in a game do we uncritically take another player's word for something? Knowledge and a sharpened intellect give citizens power.

What survives/less detectable

On a graph, if we were to plot actual corruption versus evidence of that corruption, it could turn out to be a direct relationship, shown as a straight, diagonal line. Or the graph could show a curve that indicated less and less *sign* of corruption even as it was increasing. There are indeed several reasons that as corruption grows it could become less apparent. (Recall, as a reminder, that we have defined corruption as both a trend toward less ethical people holding power and the concentration of power itself.) As we have pointed out, one of the very features of corruption that can enable it to take hold, is its ability to make itself invisible. Power can be used by individuals to conceal or obfuscate the true nature of their actions and deeds. In our case, today, it could be that it is exactly *because* of power concentration that the full truth about power concentration is not readily apparent.

Where stealth is what is intended, it will be the *best* stealth that is the hardest to spot. To know this is to have an edge in deciphering society. Interestingly, where stealth is not even intended (i.e. premeditated)—as with nature and natural selection—it will still be the things that are hardest to detect that will be the hardest to detect! (For an organism, incidentally, "hard to detect" would be a detriment if it is in the eyes of a potential mate, while an asset if in regard to a predator. Organisms are able to hide *or* advertise themselves, as needed.) Speaking generally, things that survive in any system do so because of features (like durability, camouflage, owning the media) that enable that survival. Being on the lookout for these features, I suggest, is a fruitful approach to social science as well as an interesting way to augment our understanding of the larger world.

These notions—about stealth, deception, and their outcomes—apply broadly to encroachments on liberty and democracy. If a scheme to gain control of an economy, a government apparatus, or even a foreign country, were a crude plan, then it could or would be easily exposed. It is carefully crafted plans that evade detection and go on to prevail. Part and parcel to this, one could also imagine that power-seeking individuals or aspiring tyrants would not miss the chance to learn from a study of history and, for example, not make such and such mistake again.

Corrupting incentives/motives

Searching for truth includes a need to apply the simple filter of looking for incentives. A common yardstick for the accuracy and reliability of the information we encounter is the credentials, expertise, or other specific qualifications of the source for that information. In a perfect world, we would have confidence in using this approach and would weight the value of what we read and hear to accord with it. Instead—and unfortunately—a search for truth turns out to be better served by looking at what motivates the people who provide us our information. Scrutinizing the incentives and disincentives that a source is subject to can give us a picture of how reliable their accounting is likely to be.

This evaluation process is mostly obvious and intuitive. Are a source's actions and statements linked to either financial or material gain? Has a life path led someone to become highly invested in a particular outcome? How would an individual's ambition or status factor into their choice of views? Would retaining one's job depend on adopting a certain stance? Could an individual's statement of beliefs actually expose them to harm? So if, for example, in being outspoken on a subject, an individual jeopardizes their career and goes on to become a lightning rod for criticism, they are probably speaking their truest belief, and they may, as well, have a character that is incorruptible. If, by contrast, a person seems only to gain by their views and activities, it might be a sign that they answer to a different master than the truth or an engaged conscience.

For a handful of reasons, large businesses are not likely to provide us with the most objective information. The primacy of profit-making is at the top of this list: candid truth only rarely coinciding with the most desired bottom line. Large media corporations—the predominant source for most people's news—are not wholly trustworthy when and if they have a quid pro quo with government and other insider sources, wherein they get priority access to important or breaking news in exchange for reporting what is understood to be approved. Such access could, of course, end abruptly with even a single transgression. Any commercial news source is only able to report the stories or versions of stories that their major advertisers find acceptable. Advertising dollars, in general, have the power to dictate which businesses and organizations survive in the markets that depend on this revenue. In the process they tempt many to adjust their practices or mission statements in order to court those dollars. Foundation and NGO funding follows a similar pattern. There is often more to learn about an organization or business by looking at its roster of advertisers and donors, than by other means. The documented placing of personnel in the major media by US intelligence agencies is an additional reason why the veracity of reporting from that sector should be questioned. (The proceedings of the 1975 Church Committee of the US Senate revealed this.)

To the extent to which we can identify these and other motivators, we can use them to better decide whom to trust. The familiar advice to "follow the money" is useful all by itself. In the decision tree for how to ascertain the value of information that we are exposed to, expertise, educational background, or reasoning skills are important when the individual in question can be trusted on other grounds.

It would almost be correct to say that there is a class of professional or seasoned liars in US society because people have been so heavily sorted according to personality type, values, and other pre-dispositions. While some organizations are full of people who are as honest as the day is long, others have screened for, and effectively collected, people who faithfully repeat company or agency perspectives, regardless of their relationship to facts or ethics. Acting as a market force, there is a greater demand for this latter skill set when there is more corruption—drawing additional such individuals out of the woodwork. I use the word "almost," above, because someone is not lying if they believe what they are saying, even if it is not true. At the other end of the spectrum are individuals who do have an outright intent to deceive or to conceal self-serving or criminal activity.

The witnessed capacity of a good magician to fool us provides a useful illustration of several points. It reminds us that we are foolable, for one thing—enforcing humility and keeping our minds on alert for clues to what really *is* true. And it reminds us of what a high degree of skill can account for. The skill of a magician in the hands of elites who might wish to mislead the public can explain almost any of the incongruities we may struggle with as we try to shape a picture of reality.

If the elite can be seen to be working *against* democracy, then their actions will tell us who is most likely working *for* democracy. One of the best clues, in other words, for deciding whom to trust or admire is to watch whom the elite attack—whether nations, world leaders, or domestic activist groups. This resembles the notion that "the enemy of your enemy is your friend." There are subtleties to this, but the concept has utility in helping to interpret the political landscape.

Yet another reason for caution in constructing a world view based on what one hears on the news is that major media are required to *not* reveal anything about covert government operations. Whether or not a newscaster knows the truth, such operations generally come with a cover story and talking points, which is what the public will receive—sometimes relentlessly. With a corrupted government, there may be a large portion of the foreign policy news that deserves to be subjected to this particular credibility filter.

In recent years the words "deep state" have been used publicly for the first time, potentially opening a window to thinking in new terms about levels or layers of influence in a country.

Conspiracy theories

People who investigate elites and their subculture and then expound on what they learn are often labeled as conspiracy theorists. The process of evaluating the credibility of groups such as these, which are socially marginalized, itself requires perspective gained from social systems logic. The demographic that makes up the particular conspiracy theorists is subject to its own feedback loop. Each prominent, influential, or respected figure that conspicuously eschews the group or movement makes association with it less attractive and more of a political liability to their peers or colleagues. The group then looks less credible in profile, and fewer still will choose to associate with it. The reverse would be true as well: the more respected or credentialed individuals who joined, the more would then be comfortable joining.

Interestingly, almost everyone who argues against the suspicions of conspiracy theorists does not show the telltale signs of being honest or capable intellectuals. One virtually never hears well-tempered comments that respectfully acknowledge puzzling evidence while then disagreeing with the conclusion. A readiness like this to throw the baby out with the bathwater is not something that should pass muster in academia or elsewhere. The rationality that will likely turn out to be a requirement for the survival of a habitable world must fairly evaluate whatever facts are at hand.

Attempts to play psychologist with conspiracy types is usually equally flawed with suggestions that wild ideas yield a raft of bonuses to well-being. Though nearly everyone has some motive to hold onto ideas that affirm the identity they have invested in in life, this is no more true of these subcultures than of others. In several ways it may be less true because of the significant disincentives that conspiracy theorists face. For instance, how desirable is it really to lose the respect of friends and relatives, to be ridiculed on the news and on talk shows, or to risk losing one's job or professional status? There are many ways that humans in all walks of life may not be practiced at careful reasoning, but generally it is incentives which corrupt that reasoning. These groups probably have fewer such incentives (i.e. things to gain from what they do) than their naysayers, who often actually stand to benefit financially from potshot activities. If there is supposed to be comfort in believing that evil individuals stalk the halls of power, I do not see the case for it. There is probably far more comfort—and therefore corrupting incentive—in believing we are safe in the hands of our government and that we belong to a nation of which we can be proud.

The use of the term "conspiracy theorist" as a criticism can sometimes make a valuable point, which is that it is unproductive or even irresponsible to, for instance, be habitually suspicious of government without employing the right amount of discernment. While there may be a few problems associated with individuals being too critical in this way, there are, arguably, greater negative consequences from people who are not being critical enough. A healthy and appropriate amount of scrutiny from the citizenry—it has often been proffered—could be a virtual cure-all for society's ills.

Secondhand

Built into the challenge of figuring out what to believe is the fact that almost everything we try to learn depends on secondhand information. We are all mostly in stages of taking people's word for things, in lieu of firsthand experience. We accommodate this reality by essentially learning how best to learn. While this is a highly individualized process, the universals behind it include that an accurate model of the world will increasingly find reinforcing material, just as scientific knowledge grows as an interpenetrated web of ideas. Like building trust, establishing the reliability of information is something that happens over time as we collect what we consider to be the most dependable sources and resources to draw upon. Our own success at conveying ideas or perspectives to others similarly depends on whether *we* are trusted and respected as a good and worthy source.

Piercing the persona

Unfortunately for the vision of a vital and robust democracy, the human instinct for discerning who among us is or is not honorable does not appear to be very good. A significant obstacle, for instance, to fathoming elite perfidy is being able to first accept that familiar faces of public officials or chiefs of industry are not necessarily being straight with us. Our attempts to read the character of the personalities that march across our TV screens is complicated by a number of factors.

First of all, we may only rarely have the chance to size up the face and body language of individuals who are the primary decision-makers in our country. In this day and age, even the President is not necessarily the one who decides most of what he or she announces. The people who address us with the developments of the day are usually one, two, or maybe many steps removed from those who formulate policy on any given issue. Just as a lie detector test cannot work for a second- or third-person retelling of a lie, we, in the public, will have nothing to learn in, say, attempting to judge the demeanor or motivation of a newscaster or press secretary.

Sometimes, however, a spokesperson does know more than they intend to reveal. In such a case, there will usually be less to glean or detect when statements are carefully crafted and planned than if the person is speaking extemporaneously. A previously agreed-upon decision to tell the public XYZ instead of the truth would enable the teller of the XYZ fib to be more composed and to speak with a confidence that would read as integrity or at least as assuredness. (A certain case of a General Colin Powell at the United Nations comes to mind here.) Valuable clues about what goes on behind a public persona can sometimes come in the form of a slip of the tongue or a revealing facial expression. Again, given the significance to a fair society of transparency and sound information, any chance for supplemental insight is a plus. Rarely, we may even spot an individual struggling to hold back a laugh—as you might witness, for example, with testimony presented to a congressional banking committee asking for hundreds of billions of dollars in bailouts. This would be an individual, incidentally, who may not be rehired.

One thing that can enable a person to not blush, flinch, or miss a beat in the midst of a lie is if they effectively have no conscience to betray them. Personality types that are sometimes classed as psychopaths or sociopaths are interesting for, among other things, their near absence of empathic feeling or a guiding sense of right and wrong. This specialty within psychology is acutely relevant to questions of how who gains power in society, and what they then do with that power.

More often than not, powerful people feel confident that they are doing good, even when objective evidence would indicate the opposite. Listening to such a person, we perceive the honorable self-perception! The documented human capacity for deceiving ourselves, mentioned in the previous chapter, is one thing that may be at work here, cleansing ill motives from awareness and therefore from detection.

The experience of persuasiveness, in and of itself, is something to marvel at. If we witness two skilled debaters take their turns at countering each other, it is not uncommon to bounce back and forth ourselves in who we think is right. This example highlights the fact that if we only heard either one of them on their own, then that is probably whose view we would come to believe. Through hundreds of familiar and not-so-familiar spokespeople, what we mostly hear in the mainstream media in the US is elite viewpoints. Inculcation would not be too strong a word for this sometimes seven-day-a-week cultural experience. *Comparison* is our standard way to gauge the worth of ideas.

And another question: Have "insiders"—in spite of their apparent boundless access to information—in fact entered a sort of tunnel in which they cannot know things that "outsiders" know? We should be wary of entering this tunnel along with them if it limits the breadth of our own thinking. Elite self-justifications and rationales inevitably suffuse their information environment, and content meant for public consumption mingles and merges with whatever the real story is— effectively indoctrinating elites themselves and narrowing their own world view. It is of equal importance for the conscientious citizen to guard against misinformed or misguided leaders as it is against ill-motivated ones. History offers up cautionary tales to do with both.

Philosophies

Included in the knowledge base that citizens could use to plumb or decipher the complex world of political maneuvering is a review of the philosophies that elites have adopted or championed over the years. In the bottom-up, self-organizing system of society that we have been profiling, elites exert a larger-than-average influence. If individuals who might dream about ruling the world actually *could* rule the world, then it is prudent to know something about what makes them tick.

One well-known expression of an elite value system is captured in the phrase *noblesse oblige*, defined as "the inferred responsibility of privileged people to act with generosity and nobility toward those less privileged." If this perspective has had eras of greater and lesser prominence, it would be interesting to examine the cultural factors behind those shifts. It could be my own hope that a fuller appreciation of the advantages that the wealthy and powerful accrue in the logic of social systems would lead more of them to see a rightness in this ethos. In the meantime there are other ideologies that are the more prevalent today.

While a longstanding historical perspective by the ruling classes that they were actually of superior stock should be long gone in the twenty-first century, some similarly pernicious views may have shown up in its place. There are schools of political thought, for instance, that rationalize deception as a necessary, and even worthy, means to an end, or that believe the elite are called upon to manage public perception of contemporary events as they see fit and for the public's own good. Some elites believe a nation finds its unity through the process of defining enemies or that an enemy is needed to create the cohesiveness a state requires in order to be a strong state. Some foster a black-and-white view of good and evil in the world and don't hesitate to vilify their chosen enemies. Others believe that the only rules are the rules of nature—i.e., none. If you win, then you have won—end of story. That some shocking rationalization may underlie what elites do should be kept in mind for the perspective it offers, and the caution it engenders. A majority of the elite may not even believe in the concept of a republic—of rule by the people—in spite of lip service to the idea.

Elites, like a lot of us, may be choosy in whom they admire. They identify with can-do people and may explicitly not believe that the meek deserve to inherit the earth. Some may think that strife is inevitable and a sign of healthy humanness. Imploring elites to be nice is probably not a way to change their behavior. Along these lines elites have been known to mock utopian talk as both distasteful (because it is missing the grit that they admire) and naive. In this thinking, if people choose to wear rose-colored glasses, it is their own fault when they get taken advantage of.

Some elites, and others, don't even think that Planet Earth is a keeper—requiring and deserving tending—but have hitched their dreams and dollars to terraforming Mars or engineering space colonies. Such beliefs may be the backstory to policies and practices that deface or degrade the earth.

Disclosure of specific "battle plans" or manifestos, like that of the 1971 Lewis F. Powell Jr. "Memorandum," or the 1998 Project For the New American Century document "Rebuilding America's Defenses" can jolt the citizen into realizing that society today is, in part, the fulfillment of concrete goals set by elite-oriented individuals. Audacious historic statements of intent, such as the Monroe Doctrine of 1823, in which the US declared that the entire Western Hemisphere was to be off limits to any power other than itself, are revealing of elite thinking in each era. The Bush Doctrine, of the US being entitled to preemptively invade a country that someday might be a threat, is telling in this way. Dating from the George H. W. Bush presidency, the Wolfowitz Doctrine states, in effect, that no nation shall be allowed to stand in the way of US domination. A little bit of translating, and this can be interpreted to mean that neither would moral concerns be permitted to obstruct that path.

The concept of becoming masters of the world is an inevitable kind of goal that has probably arisen over and over in pockets of culture for at least the last few hundred years. Humans are predisposed to king-of-the-hill type drives, and this aspiration can be assumed to be a theme in the culture of elites. After centuries or millennia of geostrategic games, a temptation to be the last and final winner must be significant.

It is hard to detect what codes of ethics are in place among the biggest elite players, outside of ones that may help maintain discipline and cooperation within their circles. When it comes to international relations, "might makes right" may be the statement that best matches the facts, and in the world culture of today may be a strategy that succeeds as other more ethically-constrained approaches are winnowed away. In a joint book project titled *On Western Terrorism: From Hiroshima to Drone Warfare*, Noam Chomsky and Andre Vltchek claim that imperialism by the West has resulted in fifty to fifty-five million deaths worldwide in the years since World War II. To the extent to which elites can know or anticipate the outcomes of their foreign interventions, there must be a place in their belief systems that accepts this kind of consequence. Above and beyond behavior based on ideologies of pure expediency, studies of in-group and out-group psychology do explain a great deal about the witnessed human capacity for discounting of the lives of "others," as well as for the sentiment of hatred itself.

Techniques of empire

If there are any two "contestants" we have been focusing our discussion on, they would be the elite (holding substantial individual power) and the populace (holding relatively little individual power). Strategies of and for the populace—or citizenry—will be talked about in the next two chapters. Here, a glancing review of what appear to be some elite strategies can help with the picture of how their power is both acquired and maintained. Notice that learning how big players in society use their power is something that increases the power of the learner—because, recall, we influence the world based on things such as our knowledge.

Perhaps the foremost method of gain for elites is to "capture" (or get primary control of) the apparatus of their government—which then, as a further tool, can capture the apparatus of other governments. Having control of a government gives one all the leverage that comes with its institutions, including those for making laws, running the military, determining expenditures, planning economic policy, and implementing foreign policy. When this degree of control is achieved, a large array of pathways for gain are open to an elite.

There exists an extensive playbook—with a long history in colonialism—for how to get control of another country and its resources. When it comes to overseas projection, the engineering of a coup d'état, or regime change gambit, must certainly be a standard item for a hegemonic power, even to the point of picking one of a half dozen methods. It works to the advantage of an aggressor that societies always have individuals and groups with distinct beliefs and aims. If a government is earmarked to be overthrown, strategic planners can seek out even a marginalized, disgruntled faction and bolster its power to the point where it can significantly impact that society. By providing weapons, money, intelligence, or PR cover, elites are giving away power to the proxy groups it selects. They, in effect, infiltrate a country by funneling resources to their opponent's opponents. This practice is extremely common and takes many forms. Courting bribable individuals who can be installed as oligarchs, strongmen, or other versions of a puppet leader is another step in this process.

There are a number of cruel binds that an aggressor can put a target country in to then justify an intervention. Countries that are under clandestine attack often have to modify civil liberties to fend off spying or enemy propaganda. This can be seized upon as a sign of a lack of freedom, giving the aggressor an excuse for interfering where there was none to begin with. Imperial powers also use the trick of saying that defensive acts are aggressive acts. Like the scenario of repeatedly poking one's sibling and then feigning innocent victim when they strike back, elites with enough control over information can use this and similar ploys on a target country.

An elite quest to find tactics that advance their goals could not help but come up with the idea of creating what can be thought of as a synthetic or engineered reality: details concocted or contrived to tell an incorrect story. This may involve planning and staging deceptive events but can also include disseminating narratives that are made up out of whole cloth. In this latter case, and under the right circumstances, the mere managing of information and "news" content would be vastly easier than controlling on-the-ground events in a direction to meet one's goals.

Certain elite objectives may require an enemy that doesn't really exist in the form they might like. Vociferously demonizing—or exaggerating the threat of—a person, a country, or a movement works to establish the specter of that threat in the public eye. Closely related, the technique of creating war fever through a staged attack on oneself that is blamed on an opponent has extensive historical precedent and goes by the name of a "false flag" attack, referring (in one version) to the flag that an impostor warship flies to create the ruse. Framing an enemy is the intent here. Above and beyond how irresistible employing this degree of subterfuge must be for power- or profit-seeking elites, to begin to accumulate successful examples of such operations would quickly turn it into a strategic specialty.

Sowing strife, promoting civil wars, or generally trying to get people fighting among themselves is a familiar tactic to the point that it is surprising it still works, and that populations would not spot and resist the provocations. Sometimes merely wrecking the integrity of a country achieves the goal of an imperialist, throwing it into chaos or sending it "back to the Stone Age." As Naomi Klein details in her book *The Shock Doctrine: The Rise of Disaster Capitalism*, devastation is fertile ground for opportunistic enterprises.

Individuals who are needy or in debt are in a weak bargaining position. This fact provides the centerpiece to a range of money-making strategies utilized by the elite. When people are needy, they will work for low wages and tolerate unpleasant jobs. They will not risk organizing into unions. Needy people will borrow at high interest rates or sell things at a bargain to keep their heads above water. Interest payment on debt is a major income stream for elite lenders and their institutions and the basis for many a fortune. Getting debtors in over their heads may be a path to greater gain for lenders if their "backs are covered" and the bad debt will be bought by the IMF or they are in line for a public bailout. Indebted countries will agree to sell off or privatize publicly held assets to maintain access to needed borrowing or to stay in good stead with entities they are dependent on. Borrowing by countries is often initially via a propped-up leader as part of a racket—the whole population becoming indebted in the process. The losing end of the positive feedback power equation is that the worse things get, the worse things get. A cycle of debt and dependence leading to more debt and dependence illustrates this.

According to economist Paul Craig Roberts in his book *The Failure of Laissez Faire Capitalism*, "Western financial institutions . . . have acquired the ability to manipulate prices in equity, bond, currency, and commodity markets." This is fully equivalent to having insider information with all that that can net. These institutions, and the individuals who make them up, undoubtedly also have some control over business cycles and speculative bubbles, enabling them to buy, and cash in, at opportune times. Business cycles provide a periodic opportunity for flush individuals to scoop up assets of people who have been broken in the downswing.

Elites in the US are generally very attentive to maximizing their influence in Congress. Beyond efforts to fill the seats with candidates of their choosing, a substantial private industry exists to conceive, compose, and then attempt to pass legislation in both the US House and Senate. The well-known ALEC (American Legislative Exchange Council) bill factory is a part of this. It could be argued that this kind of initiative is a parallel to lobbying by citizen interest groups. One difference would be in the power arrayed behind the corporate and elite version of it.

If there is anything more serviceable for elites than the making of laws, it would be to control their selective enforcement. Perhaps the most significant arrow in the elite quiver is an ability to influence the justice system of a country with its jurisdiction over who is and is not investigated, indicted, prosecuted, or convicted for crimes. If and when someone knows they are above the law, then that becomes an enticement to plan and carry out illegal acts.

The effectiveness of any and all of the strategies and approaches mentioned here is, as always, environment dependent. The same methods that would win in one societal context could lead to losing in a different context—such as one with greater transparency, a higher level of education, functioning accountability, or a less consolidated media.

We talked, above, about how elites in a corrupted government may attempt to "capture" and control another country that they hope to benefit from. If this attempt at control was over a non-wealthy country, chances are that it would be barefaced, or even be in the form of an invasion. But if and when a powerful country seeks to control a peer, then stealth would be required. This could include the familiar steps of finding factions to promote and fund, then ultimately installing decision-makers that favor the outside entity. A storyline can be pieced together that shows Canada, Australia, Japan, European countries, and others, slowly and increasingly yielding to the sway of the United States. But what about the susceptibility of the US itself to this kind of subversion? Could it be subject to control by other countries? The apparent influence of the state of Israel on the US Congress, including over its foreign aid expenditures, suggests that the US has been captured to some extent by foreign elites. Some individuals claim that the US is beholden to Britain and to *its* most powerful cliques. But exactly who and what would have been "taken over" in the US if its democracy had already succumbed to influence by internal private interests? Who is controlling whom? Could controllers be from multiple countries or even have no allegiance to any nation? Can countries control each other at the same time—and what would that be called? All of this resembles the biologists' concepts of parasitism and mutualism, but with the complicating difference that a country is divisible into parts—into its separate and independently willful citizens.

Scrutiny/prudence

A significant difference between investigating in the natural sciences versus in the social sciences is that—beyond habitual avoidance behavior by organisms, where it exists—natural phenomena have no capacity to willfully hide from the investigator. For the same reasons that actions of humans may be hidden from each other, including from the broader public, they are also hidden (usually by default, not intent) from academic inquirers. An eye for understanding the filters that information is subject to, and by which it can disappear (e.g. be classified) or be altered (e.g. spun), is a partial remedy for this. Included here is the challenge to understand the subtlest filter of all, the inquirer's own identity and belief systems. This is also more of a factor for social scientists than for natural scientists because of the strength with which people hold political opinions and national allegiances that may encroach on their objectivity.

The basis for citizens being watchdogs of their government and its leaders is familiar. Several additional considerations for applying that scrutiny could include the following. 1) If a government has lied to the public in the past, it is smart to be alert to current and future lies. 2) The documented worst act or acts by a government can be used as a measure of what it is correct to suspect that it could do again. 3) Another reasonable perspective is that what the US government, say, does overseas to other populations, it could also do at home. 4) Surprisingly, there is a reflexive tendency to take government officials at their word. They, however, should be expected to provide evidence for any important or consequential claims that they make—as would be standard in a court of law or a scientific publication.

When it comes to assessing potential threats posed by new developments in society, a simple matrix can be consulted. We can ask,

"How bad would a bad consequence be?" and "What are the chances that that could happen?" The "threat" is the one times the other: the potential consequences times the likelihood of it happening or being true. Like the thinking behind the precautionary principle, our care, concern, research, or attention should be commensurate with a potential danger. This applies to weighing the wisdom of things like sending radioactive material into orbit, taunting a nuclear-armed country, or tolerating the total surveillance of the phone and Internet records of a population. Individual choices like becoming a soldier should likewise be considered with great care. Killing or being killed are both the highest order of consequence. It is an interesting question why young men and women do not seem to investigate more deeply the legitimacy of the wars they enlist to fight in or the history of past wars and interventions.

Somewhere at the intersection of prudence and historical literacy is the notion that we consult the advice of great people who have gone before us. The cultural record is full with quotations that remind us of standards we can aspire to, things to be on guard against, and enduring wisdom of the ages.

Where would it most likely lead?

We began this chapter by wondering aloud what it is that stops positive feedback power accumulation if and when it gets started. In the US there is no question but that this cyclical process is both underway and in an advanced state. Statistics on wealth inequality seem to be revised upward on an almost monthly basis. Numbers from the Washington Center for Equitable Growth in a 2019 report show the net worth of the top 1 percent of the population to be greater than that of the bottom 90 percent. According to Les Leopold of the Labor Institute the average CEO-to-starting-worker pay ratio in the top 100 firms has gone from 45-to-1 in 1970, to on the order of 800-

to-1 in 2016. Leopold also shares that in 2009 the top ten hedge fund managers made an average wage of $900,000/hour! (Measuring wealth is much easier than measuring power, and wealth statistics can often serve as a reasonable proxy for power distribution.) Globally, a January 2020 Oxfam report states that 2,153 billionaires have the same wealth as 60 percent of the world's population, or 4.6 billion people. Attention certainly has been focused on this growing inequality by a range of scholars, activists, and politicians. The link between wealth and its capacity to undermine a healthy democracy has rightly been center stage in this discussion and debate. Exactly because of this spotlight, however, it would be equally talked about if there had been anything new to substantially change the state of affairs.

Pushback from the citizenry is the force that we would expect to arise to stop excessive power accumulation. Other alternatives—some meant to intentionally stretch the imagination—could include the following: A system change from feedback logic to a law of diminishing returns for additional gains in wealth as some limiting factor sets in; an initiative to rectify inequality that originated from the elite themselves; a collapse scenario for the wealthy from an increased focus on short-term thinking; infighting among elites in which they sabotage each other; a decline of military might relative to other countries as boondoggle-style contracting becomes the norm; or a massive electronic failure that wiped out digital records of assets. Sticking with the initial possibility, unless and until there is a marked intervention from the public to challenge the causes of inequality, we remain in a pattern where power can be used to advance itself, enabling it to continue to concentrate.

One sober, and even disquieting, question before us is, "What characteristics would society be likely to have in a state of advanced and advancing power accumulation?" Up to a point, it would have the characteristics we see around us in the US and much of the West today, with traits, dynamics, and playing field changes similar to some of those we have been describing. These include features like the subordination of government to corporate interests, an increasing failure of the judicial system to deliver justice, expansion of overseas military presence, militarized police forces, censorship on multiple fronts, greater secrecy, and more surveillance.

The path from there—or from here—would depend on how a series of overlapping and interrelated dynamics play out:

Elites can be expected to use the power they have. They are in the odd situation of it being too easy to shape society to their wishes, with most being unwilling to forgo the use of that power. As elite power grows, individuals in the rest of society become poorer, have less agency, are less secure, and experience a decline in well-being. In response they become increasingly motivated to act to challenge the source of these problems. When things are bad for the citizenry, people also have less to lose, and therefore fewer psychological constraints on their behavior. The more that people challenge elite practices and power, the more the elite will act to counter this. The elite know that a percentage of the population would be immune to indoctrination and would never cooperate with rule by the few. The elite can be expected to anticipate a stage where their growing power, with its increasing dispossession of the population, would lead to civil unrest. Standard methods of persuasion or placation could progress to coercion, suppression, oppression, or even incarceration, depending. With the "gloves off," elite moves could sharply affect public perception and opinion and lead to a sudden and acute situation for the government.

When all of the above is charted or plotted, there is a theoretical divide that can be identified between whether or not the awareness and response of the populace arrives in time, and in the right amount, to succeed at halting elite momentum. If a counterforce to the elite does not succeed, the society that comes to pass will be one in which the elite have carte blanche to do as they please (though probably contesting among themselves), and further attempts to challenge their power would be for naught. The public in this state may be a mix of somnambulant, resistant but powerless, strategically cooperating, surrendered to their fate, or integrating into an elite worldview.

Presumably, some elites would want to avoid the risk of rebellion or the inconvenience of repression, and so would choose to willingly temper their pursuit of power. But those who tried to do this would face the prospect of being eclipsed by others who did not. It could happen that the uppermost fraction of elites reach an agreement to all hold back on the exercise of their power, but it would require the right incentives and disincentives to create the cooperation that would entail. There are a handful of recognized reasons elites should want to maintain a semblance of a middle class in society such as that producers need a public capable of buying their goods. A prosperous public could also afford to borrow money or to gamble in financial markets—both with advantages for elites. And shared prosperity would contribute to creating a generous tax base for the elite to draw from.

A "problem," as we have mentioned, is a subjective thing. The case can be made that when there is a maximum of democracy, there are a minimum of problems because the greatest number of people have had input into the decisions shaping society. So, if the elite were to lock in control and shut out the wishes and "vote" of the wider public (creating, in other words, a minimum of democracy), it would be a world flooded with problems and fraught with difficulties as understood by the greatest number of people. It should not surprise us if this concentration in power also corresponds with a state of environmental crisis, due to the profit available from the harvesting, liquidation, and abuse of natural systems. Human health would be expected to decline as well for reasons having to do with our acute dependence on a sound and unsullied natural world.

To the question of how citizens can stop excessive power accumulation, the next two chapters look for answers. In the meantime, there is an important distinction to ferret out between disruption of a democracy from inside a country, versus disruption that originates from the outside.

Large scale, small scale

I have speculated that the most consequential social system pattern in human history is that the acquisition of power follows positive feedback logic. The picture of how this takes place includes both that factions grow in power within the confines of a society, *and* that powerful groups will grow by the same kind of feedback cycle through interactions with other societies. These two modalities are usually found operating together.

My reading of history tells me that fair and stable societies have emerged many times, and that this has been true from antiquity through to recent decades. How many of these harmonious societies have been disrupted from the inside as powerful factions grew up within them, and how many have been disrupted, instead, from the outside? My guess is that the greater percentage have been disrupted from the outside by invasion or by intentional infiltration. A focus on how to prevent corruption from gaining a foothold within one's own country may be only a small part of the challenge for nations of the world today. Ever since a motive existed to attack another group in order to steal pigs, land, women, gold, or coltan, there has been the puzzle of how to repel outside aggression, whether overt or covert.

Researchers like William Blum, author of *Killing Hope: US Military and CIA Interventions Since World War II*, can tell you how the US, in the last sixty-plus years, has derailed the egalitarian experiments of many dozens of countries. Worthy societies have repeatedly been wrecked or wiped out by the US and other contemporary imperialist powers, just as they were wrecked or wiped out by the Mongol armies of the thirteenth century, or the Spanish Conquistadors of the sixteenth. The pattern is an old one. The infiltrating or invading entity gains in power and wealth at the expense of the "host" country, whose autonomy is undercut in the process. The advantages that enable this to be carried out successfully are all familiar ones and have to do with social inventions like warfare strategies and economic maneuvers, as well as with degrees of technological sophistication, numbers of personnel, motivational rhetoric, and the like. Not only does the border of a nation not confine the exercise of power by a powerful group, but to the extent to which laws are ill-defined or unenforceable internationally, there may be added temptations to operate abroad. An addendum to the thesis that equality within a society is a vulnerable state subject to take-over by a faction, is that the integrity and well-being of a nation is also vulnerable to aggression and take-over from external groups that have grown by the same cyclical accretion of power. If even one nation or global faction becomes excessively powerful and adopts the tactics of a bully, then the consequences for other countries and populations, both near and far, may be substantial.

Life-spans

An additional culture-shaping pattern, which we have so far skirted, is the differential survival of humans themselves (wherein nonrandom processes determine the longevity of individuals). When differential survival relates to changes in gene frequencies in the gene pool, it is classed as part of natural selection. But when humans end up leading longer or shorter lives because of what they believe and how they choose to act, then this is part of the accounting of culture. A component of our explanation for which cultural things survive is whether the individuals who are predisposed to make specific contributions to culture survive bodily. A long life-span means more years in which to make one's unique mark on culture. A shorter life-span results in less of what that individual would contribute.

In a war of aggression, the population of the victim country may be highly motivated to defend their families, culture, or the country's sovereignty. A case can be made that it is especially brave, capable, righteous, knowledgeable, or honor-bound individuals who are the first to volunteer to fight. The selective deaths of such individuals changes the makeup of a culture, and hence its trajectory in history.

Around the world, people who oppose elites can do so from the pulpit, the ivory tower, in the media, on the Internet. These individuals may run risks if their threat is substantial. It is a high-stakes game to challenge certain powerful people. Remember that ruthlessness can be a winning trait in a corrupted society, and that such individuals sort themselves into collaborating with each other. Those who stand up to elites—besides losing agency by being slandered, fired, censored, or locked up—may also face a graver fate. Depending on the country, the setting, or the era, opponents of an elite can lose their lives via death squads, drone strikes, a potentate's decree, or via a plotted assassination. History is full of episodes and incidents of such power contests with this consequence. It is a major dynamic in shaping culture, and in particular for locking in dominance when a group becomes above the law.

Along these same lines, a current epidemic in the killing of environmental activists in contested locales around the world speaks to a standard corruption dynamic: by definition, whoever is capable of getting away with such a crime is someone who has acquired substantial power, if only, in some cases, by the removal of law and order (power over them) in that given country.

Activists' battles can be won or lost on the strengths—such as charisma or leadership—that are extant within their membership, as well as on numbers of participants, which will generally decline if dangers increase. The future is determined by who can shape it, and by how much.

Evolution

Readers may notice that so far I have not used the phrase "cultural evolution" in this discussion. The use of the term invites being drawn into a recondite academic analysis, emphasizing methods of cultural transmission that can sometimes be dry and/or mathematical. It also tempts the reader to look for parallels with biological evolution, where there may only be a few. One thing that biological and cultural evolution have in common is differential survival. In both cases many possibilities are narrowed down to that which remains. The evolution or propagation of culture is actually less like natural selection than it is like Lamarckism—an early theory of biological evolution in which *acquired* characteristics were what were thought to be passed on. In biological evolution, traits of an organism are replicated with extreme fidelity, and novelty comes about primarily through random processes. As human culture evolves, the creation of its novelty is directed by human preferences, and the content of that culture is an ongoing mix of both replication (copying) and invention. The full array of traits that were responsible for the human ability to make culture represented a watershed moment for the design capabilities of biological evolution on Earth. When natural selection hit on the culture-making aptitude of humans, it had struck gold, so to speak. Suddenly an organism existed that could devise "adaptations" to meet almost any new circumstance—for the human line, utterly upstaging the traditional route to adaptations and to increasing fitness. And the rest is, actually, history.

The broadest meaning of the word "evolution" describes a process where, in a given system, each new state that arises depends on the previous state and sets the stage for the next state. As things evolve, there is cause and there is effect, seamlessly relating what is to what becomes. The activity of deciphering and divining outcomes (which is our mantra here) *is* studying the evolution of culture, aka cultural evolution: it is looking at the logic that takes any part of society from one state to the next. An intimate knowledge of the details of causes and effects for culture increases one's ability to plan in order to make things happen, taking part in guiding the path of this evolution.

CHAPTER FOUR

Nuts, Bolts, and Social Change

"When one comes to think of it, there are no such things as divine, immutable or inalienable rights. Rights are things we get when we are strong enough to make good our claim on them."

—Helen Keller

It is common, in my experience, to hear people say, "The world would be so much better off if *only* we would strive to be more like nature: in balance, interconnected, harmonious." My response is usually something to the effect that the reason we have the problems we do is exactly *because* we are being like nature. When natural ecosystems are in balance and humming along with a diversity of inhabitants, it is not due to a willful generosity or restraint on any organism's part. It is instead explainable as a compact equilibrium of tautologically selfish individuals who are each pushing at the limits of their potential habitat. They are doing the best that they can—which is only so good. One reason their populations remain relatively stable, and no species takes over, is that they each are highly specialized for an ecological niche. The better an organism is at prospering in one niche, the worse it will generally be at coping with an alternative, adjacent niche. So, side-by-side diversity, usually in interpenetrated habitats and with a high degree of interdependence, is the result—which, it is true, is a kind of harmony. Certain of humanity's problems originate with the fact that we have broken the confines of our original primordial niche—a niche that long ago kept our impacts in check. Natural selection ultimately gave us the means to effectively invent adaptations, rather than relying on largely random processes to give us one possible new capability at a time, as other organisms do. We are so clever that we can live in almost any terrestrial environment, have vanquished most things that would prey on us, and can reap or manage our "prey" in hitherto unimagined quantities. We developed the ability to magnify our will through the use of tools and inventions to the point where we are currently operating beyond the carrying capacity of our available habitat. Over-impact can happen in the wild to a different degree, but in such cases the despoiling organisms are adapted with the ability to move on to new habitats. Moving on, most would agree, is not a choice that is available to humans. Every other organism on Earth *can* seek to maximize its welfare, yet will only meet with limited success. Humans now have so much capability that they meet with too much success. We have outgrown the niche that integrated us into a natural equilibrium. Since nature does not constrain us, we are left to constrain ourselves. The notion of humans no longer being eligible to inhabit the Garden of Eden and follow the way of nature is actually quite an apt one.

There is an additional reason that we cannot expect to emulate the natural world. In nature—where there is no right or wrong, and no rules other than natural laws—there are an immense number of casualties. I feel that a worthy goal and orientation of society is to minimize "casualties." The experiment of civilization could be described as an agreement to all cooperate to attain something that would not be possible otherwise—to create, in this case, a sustainable mode of living that looks out for the welfare of all.

Addressing these higher social aspirations, as well as ecological facts of life, means choosing to change or adapt our personal behavior. A bit more complicated, however, it also can call for changing the behavior of those whose actions we disagree with. This latter undertaking would be a delicate mission indeed, since everyone has something different to say about who is, or is not, going about things the right way. What is and is not sustainable can be defined scientifically, but almost everything else about how humans choose to shape their society is subjective. Differing opinions abound. Each of us advocating for our own personal vision, or for an agreed upon collective vision, is what a self-organizing social system ultimately distills down to. Paraphrasing Helen Keller, the society we believe in is what we get only when we are strong enough to make good our claim to it.

In one hundred words or less, a recap of our main storyline tells us that individuals in society pursue well-being, and some humans are so successful at this that they accumulate a substantial amount of power, which can be used to gain more power. Under certain circumstances individuals with few moral constraints will do better than others. Enhanced power also means a greater ability to persuade and to influence the behavior of others. Members of society with proportionally more power see the advantage of collaborating with each other to progressively fashion a world in which they succeed. They may commandeer the apparatus of government, including for both domestic and foreign policies, to further their interests.

This dynamic has left us, in much of the West, with an overabundance of power in the hands of a small and increasingly supranational subculture. This has also left us with a panoply of world problems that, in many cases, are traceable to the lack of leverage people have to adequately advance their own welfare. The universe of proposed solutions to these problems is huge, and we will barely touch on that expanse here. But few of these frequently inspired alternatives will get their day in the sun if we do not get our ship pointed in the right direction first. We must see our problems and challenges accurately, understanding not only the magnitude of the corruption that appears to have hijacked civilized society in the West, but also the underlying mechanisms that account for this kind of distortion of democracy.

(Incidentally, the most fundamental reason that everything in nature is in relative balance is that negative feedbacks in systems stick around, while positive feedbacks resolve to a different outcome over time. One is innately stable and hence enduring; the other unstable and destined to end. By way of illustration, nature probably didn't look very balanced during the decades in which a fungus responsible for the American chestnut blight killed an estimated 3 billion trees in the eastern US. And with the trees gone, balance was more apparent.)

Response to environments/making choices

For individuals interested in social change toward an egalitarian society, there are many strategic considerations that follow directly from the patterns and processes described in the preceding chapters. The same lens that we have used to look at the origin of our predicaments in society can be used to help find our way out of those self-same predicaments. The behavior of so-called complex nonlinear systems, which describe many aspects of society, is nothing if not full of surprises. A "linear" system would mean that variables in it have a proportional relationship to each other. Nonlinear systems, on the other hand, include feedbacks, thresholds, buffering (insensitivity to change), tendencies to bifurcate or to go "chaotic," and more. With knowledge as leverage, this array of system behaviors can be referenced to help in bringing about desired change. Intervening in a human social system in the right way, with the right force, and at the right time can, in theory, redirect it almost effortlessly toward a new and different state. This brings to mind the story of how the single act of reintroducing wolves to Yellowstone National Park, after seventy years of absence, led to the transformation of a wide range of ecosystems, in what is referred to as a trophic cascade. The skill and austerity of motion of a martial artist also hints at how we can approach change for society. On a more technical note, tweaking even the simplest rules of action in what are called cellular automata demonstrate how small changes yield sometimes dramatic and surprising outcomes. And one more example: A fashion model wearing a pair of L.L. Bean boots one time on a runway led to an utter avalanche of orders that continued to overstretch the company even four years later.

The essence of change in society will turn out to be an interplay between humans changing the cultural landscape and the cultural landscape changing humans.

As we have mentioned, variable environments will evoke variable responses. To the extent to which it could engineer it, natural selection would always have given an organism the capacity to act appropriately in multiple different environments. One classic example of nature's response to environments is the tree that grows in an open field to become round, spreading, and voluminous. The very same genetic stock grown amidst a stand of other trees will be tall, slender, and have foliage only at its crown. Along with a handful of other firsts, humans almost certainly rank at the top among organisms for this kind of ingrained versatility. Our related gifts include the ability to detect subtle features of our physical and social circumstances and to assess and weigh the potential outcomes of the behavior choices that are available to us. We are well equipped to respond differently and appropriately to each new environment we find ourselves in.

In the simple model we have been using to evaluate society, we said that humans act to optimize their well-being by weighing the perceived costs and benefits of available choices. Unlike nature, which calculates real costs and benefits of behavior choices with the carefully defined concept of an organism's "fitness," our perceived costs and benefits are not tethered to anything objective. The personal and subjective perception of our circumstances is all that matters in guiding choices. If those choices lower our biological fitness and lead to our decline, that is a matter for the calculus of natural selection and gene survival. Society, as we are analyzing it, is a separate system, and the costs and benefits that matter to us—calculated by our psychology—are subjective ones.

If the universal motive for human behavior is defined as increases in well-being, then what happens when a person acts altruistically? The concept of altruism rightly factors prominently in discussions about the character and quality of society and of our prospects for getting along peaceably. Most people would agree that such a tendency to be generous beyond keeping score is invariably a positive factor in society. For the sake of parsimony in our social system model, we will define altruistic acts in an unconventional way as being a win for both the giver and the receiver (or for the giver and *presumably* the receiver). In fact, we will go one step further and define all human choices as the subjective best choice from among those that are available. We are, therefore, *always* making our best choice—the choice we want. In the case of altruism, for example, we choose it because it is its own reward. In some instances a best choice for an individual is, in effect, a least worst choice. The key idea in this definition is that we make the "best choice from among those available." If during wartime there is a draft, a young person may have a choice of fighting overseas or going to jail. We may choose to hold onto a stressful job instead of enduring a lowered standard of living. People may face a choice between a less-than-perfect marriage or being single. Based on our perceptions, we decide what is a best choice.

Using a computer analogy, we described culture as the output from our output-device bodies. Working in conjunction with this is the decision-making capability of our mind and psychology, which we pictured as our composite, biological, central processing unit, system and applications software, and memory storage. One distinct way our human version of these is different from most computers is that our CPU and software both learn and self-upgrade as experience teaches us new things. This learnability includes the way that socialization and enculturation contribute to shaping our belief and value systems, which go on to prominently inform our life choices. Life experience also perpetually adds data to our memory banks, which we can refer to when making decisions. The mind's conclusions about the nature of our circumstances and available choices, then, are the equivalent of a calculation, or the execution of an algorithm. The mind and our psychology figure out what our next contribution to culture will be.

Change inner/outer

This has been a long detour from talking about change in society. But where this is leading is that making a change to culture by our actions can change other people in two ways. It can bring out a new response from a fixed "repertoire" of responses, as in the tree example. Or it can change the mind, changing the way our psychology weighs and perceives the culture around it, so that we "calculate" differently. An example of this second pattern can be found in the crafty way that Mark Twain's character, Tom Sawyer, gets friends to paint his fence for him, so he can go fishing instead—with them seeing the job as a privilege instead of a chore!

There is promise in both of these paths to social change. A given change to the cultural environment can bring out a latent response naturally. Or, a "learning" experience can change the way we value and prioritize things and, in theory, lead us to respond differently even to the same old culture. The most familiar mode for adjusting the behavior of citizens is to create incentives. This falls into the first category, an external change that brings out a different response. Education, being inspired by something, or having a change of heart generally are the second category. This can be thought of as change by changing the outside, or change by changing the inside, respectively. As an example, the actual dollar amount for an item can change, or the price can stay the same but we learn something that leads us to see more or less worth in the item at that price.

Wild cards

The elite may have some hard cold numbers behind their accumulated power and wealth, giving them an apparent advantage. But for individuals questing for a fair and sustainable world, there are at least three significant wild cards that are in play in society, two of which we have just touched on. First, the fact that humans are so acutely sensitive to variables in their environment means there is no telling where any particular external change could lead. Second, our perception of what is desirable is highly mutable meaning that (through an inner change) nearly anything could come to be identified with pride, status, or well-being. The third wild card is that power, itself, is a multifaceted, complex, and even mysterious thing, which can be mustered almost out of thin air when social circumstances are right.

Redistribution of power

Imagine the difference between having to find one hundred solutions to one hundred problems, or, potentially, solving all of them with one change. This may not be quite the arithmetic of our current social challenge, but I venture to say it is not far off the mark. The one change and promise I refer to would be a redistribution of power to bring us into alignment with the essential definition of democracy. A vision of redistributing power and wealth has been with organized human social groups for a long time. If there is nothing new in this aspiration, then there deserves to be something new toward its fulfillment.

Beyond matters that relate directly to wealth or power distribution, humanity faces other kinds and classes of problems, some of which we both have examined or will touch on. But is it not a safe, efficient, and prudent approach to address the inequality issue first and foremost, and thereby reveal its relationship to other problems? So how do we redistribute power, or "devolve power downward," as Naomi Kline says more formally? How do we create a society of equally influential individuals and restore the democracy in the US that appears to have faltered so badly?

Elites in think tanks, councils, corporate board rooms, and alphabet agencies most certainly engage in a creative process of conceiving plans for their own advancement and for the fulfillment of their vision of what society should be. Simultaneous to this is the ongoing work of those with a different vision for the world that explicitly includes the welfare of all beings. As an exercise in trying to fathom this counterpoising effort originating from the broader public, author and entrepreneur Paul Hawken began to count the number of groups and organizations dedicated to working toward a just and sustainable world. His tally soared to, and beyond, a million, as he chronicles in *Blessed Unrest: How the Largest Social Movement in History Is Restoring Grace, Justice, and Beauty to the World*, his book on the subject. A remarkable feature of these groups, Hawken points out, is that their missions are almost wholly complementary, even with the vast diversity they represent. While the world of creative activism is somewhat more fractious now than it was in 2007 when his book was written, the theme is still a strong one.

If there are so many people at work on this collective project, it is reasonable to ask why we nonetheless face the crises we do and why the trend of power accumulation continues to reel out of control. One answer to this question is that, without such efforts, things might be worse now than they currently are. There are other answers too. Social justice and environmental groups tend to be occupied with putting out "wildfires," addressing one pressing emergency after another. Because of power issues, most of the projects that these groups conceive sadly remain unimplemented or only partially implemented. There may also be a temptation to set smaller goals in order to have at least some measurable successes. Initiatives that truly threaten the elite may be actively thwarted through numerous means, leaving, ironically, surviving organizations that only chip at the edges of the largest problems. Then again, collectively, such efforts may have resulted in us being on or near the threshold of an important social tipping point.

For individuals who are used to thinking in this way, a goal of equalizing power and wealth can be approached as if it were a design challenge or design problem—which itself can be divided into several related puzzles. Not unlike the task our Founding Fathers undertook so long ago, a fair society can be designed from scratch with free rein on all the elements that make up the design. In their case, the original US Constitution was the document that cataloged these design features. Far more complicated, and less theoretical, is the project of figuring out how to get from where we are today, in a corrupted democracy, to where we would like to be, with relatively balanced political and economic power. Along with the followup goal of then keeping society in an equitable state, this is an endeavor that calls for the utmost in creativity, vision, and intellectual acuity, among other traits. Grist for this mill is provided in the balance of this chapter, surveying strategic considerations, potential stumbling blocks, design features, and subtle dynamics.

Design collaboration/competition

The exploration and development of ideas for how to create a fair society could be taken from its most common forums in activists' living rooms and NGO offices to the public sphere itself. In a model similar to Wikipedia, there could be a collaborative project to solve the core dilemmas of society. Like open-source software or crowd-sourcing, collective designing and trouble-shooting is a powerful way to harness human creativity and genius to a goal. Such a venture could also be set up as an international competition, not unlike the computer tournaments organized by Robert Axelrod in 1985 that shed so much light on the Iterated Prisoner's Dilemma. People who love to solve puzzles love to solve puzzles! The challenge of solving the human predicament could be enticing. Such an initiative might generate its own publicity and take important ideas mainstream as journalists were drawn to report on something new and different. The competition, or online design collaboration, could pose the specific question of how to get from a state of social inequality to a vital and stable democracy that was immune to corrupting influence or to positive feedback loops which concentrate power. A simpler project that lent itself more easily to computer modeling would be to design a corruption-proof democracy from scratch. Proposed models would be launched and observed to see which features succeeded or failed at sustaining equity in the "society."

Academics, game enthusiasts, and other individuals who are engaged in simulating culture with mathematical and computer models may well have the biggest head start in understanding the subtleties that play into design problems like these. Their knowledge needs to be tapped. (Agent-based social simulation, or ABSS, is the professional rubric that covers this approach.) An attempt to clarify what the core dilemmas of society are would quickly come up against questions like "How corrupted has the world become?" This discussion itself would need to consider such things as the paradox of secrecy, in which something that is intended to be secret cannot be readily observed in order to be evaluated. Angles like this would rightly deepen the analysis, improving in stages the quality of the collaboration or competition.

Modeling alternatives

Among the most elegant approaches to social change is simply to create an alternative and let it speak for itself. Whether a local currency, a conflict resolution method, or an intact fully-functioning alternative town or country, if the virtues of such experiments become known, then people, as they do, will copy, disseminate, and expand on the example. Instead of focusing on *stopping* something, the focus can be on starting something that may subsequently put an older practice out of business. Elites, unfortunately, are well aware of the persuasive—and in their eyes, often subversive—power of this kind of example. Historically, they have countered these relentlessly, in some cases by buying up and shelving competing patents, in others by invading even the tiniest countries, such as Grenada or Haiti, who attempt to implement fair governance. This dynamic of change by example is one of the most exciting and hopeful patterns currently playing out in society. The profusion of positive alternatives threatens to be great enough to overwhelm any attempts at suppressing them, and to allow an honest chance for people to compare and contrast what they see.

Avenues for change

Voting, publicly protesting, and appealing to our elected representatives are the most familiar and time-honored channels for making our voices heard here in the US. Each of these has been weakened for the population at large in recent decades as elites have adjusted the playing field to favor themselves. Elites, for instance, can and do own and program voting machines in the modern day United States, and there is evidence they have used this access fraudulently on multiple occasions. (See Jonathan D. Simon and Mark Crispin Miller, for example.) Elites have greater access to things such as redistricting strategies and have codified numerous winner-take-all type advantages in US election and voting rules, including debate protocols. Incremental growth—a logical kind of growth—of alternative parties, is all but impossible currently in the US.

Public and street protest has a long and dramatic history worldwide and, notably, in the US, with such memorable expressions of public will as the occasion of Martin Luther King Jr.'s "I Have a Dream" speech at the Lincoln Memorial in 1963. Particularly since the 1999 World Trade Organization protests in Seattle, Washington, elites have successfully put a damper on this venerable practice that the Founding Fathers believed they had secured the protection of. Phalanxes of Darth Vader-like police, tear gas, "free speech zones" (also called protest pens), plus the experience of being ignored regardless of turnout, together change the perceived costs of gathering publicly to petition the government for redress of grievances.

It is well known that total dollars of campaign spending is the primary factor in determining the outcome of elections to Congress and to many of the other offices charged with representing the citizenry in the US. Once elected, legislators are subject to lobbying that is, again, proportional to dollars, instead of to the input of constituents. The already small power associated with being one constituent's voice out of, sometimes, hundreds of thousands per representative is further diminished by these realities.

We are delving, here, into avenues for effecting change, but this initial inventory is not encouraging.

Our behavior in the marketplace is also a chance to send a message to others via making changes to the cultural environment in which they act. Purchasing and investing are two examples. Wherever our dollars are spent, someone who wants to be on the receiving end of those dollars will notice. If the cause and effect of this dynamic was fully appreciated and utilized by citizens, it could be on par with or exceed voting as a means for expressing our will. Organized and well-publicized versions of this, such as boycotts, buycotts, or shareholder activism, can have significant impacts.

Less recognized is our role in the marketplace of employment choices. Just as all of the actions in our lives add to become our personal contribution to the makeup of society and culture, the time we spend at work is a part of this tally. When choosing employment, we can intentionally support and take part in things we endorse and believe in. If we do not use our values as criteria in choosing a job, we give up the chance to have this additional kind of influence in the world.

Civil disobedience/non-cooperation

The subject of civil disobedience and nonviolent resistance is a large one. As strategies against aggression or oppression, these methods have some complex dynamics that can and have filled whole books on the topic. Civil disobedience is the act of consciously breaking a law in order to answer to a higher law. An "informed conscience" may see things in society that demand personal and bodily intervening, irrespective of laws which that may violate. But such acts can set an awkward precedent since others may have their own notion of higher laws they, too, would like to follow. The witnessing public will make a judgment on the difference between a frivolous or a principled action. The burden, here, is on the civil disobedience activist to clarify the reason behind their specific action. Gandhi spoke of nonviolent resistance as having the goal of transforming others. Psychology, then, is keenly at play. Feeling and showing respect for the humanity of one's opponent—fundamentally the nonviolent part—is a natural prerequisite to changing minds, and thus behavior. The converse—hating or disrespecting an opponent—hardens their resistance to a change in point of view. Sometimes direct actions resemble theater and will be effective or not, based on how compelling the "drama" is. Poise, timing, conviction, and the "script" are among the elements that may be decisive in the success of an action. Destruction of property as part of a plan is risky but has its place, while harm to others loses the whole battle. Personal suffering, Gandhi says, is a powerful potential vehicle for transforming others.

Actions like the civil rights lunch counter sit-ins in Alabama in the early 1960s were as effective as they were only because of the discipline of, and 100 percent cooperation among, the participants. If even one Black person had succumbed to being shoved by shoving back, then the press reports and consequent public perception could have been very different than they were. The need for adherence to pacifist methods makes such protests an easy target for instigators or provocateurs. One individual paid to throw a brick through a Starbucks' window can completely undo an attempt to educate the public on an important subject and to gain sought-after allies. This logic leaves activists in a handicapped position when it comes to planning. Small group actions are one way to get around this. Preemptively renouncing violence can sometimes work.

Non-cooperation—a variant of civil disobedience—is another strategy for countering corrupted government. Like throwing a spanner in the works, the apparatus of private co-option of a democracy will falter if enough people refuse to pay taxes, manufacture weapons of war, repeat a known lie, or cooperate in unethical acts. Non-co-operation often means breaking some law or risking losing one's job, presenting sometimes large disincentives for such acts of resistance. Ironically, when channels for change are relatively open, non-cooperation can look too much like anarchy or lawlessness; yet when channels have closed and a time for action is urgent, non-cooperation may land you in jail or out on the street. In any case, for non-cooperation to be effective, large numbers of people need to take part. What percentage of soldiers or police, for example, would have to disobey orders in order to stop a war, or prevent a crackdown on protesters? Does a tipping point phenomenon come into play? In coups d'état throughout history, a dynamic has played out with armed individuals needing to choose, sometimes very quickly, which side to align with. The threat to the power structure of military rebellion is so great that firing squads have sometimes been the punishment— and thereby a disincentive to others.

Most people would agree that defending ourselves and our loved ones from physical harm justifies physical force in response. Pacifist philosophy is often challenged on this point. Under what scenario might there be more gain in suffering harm, and even death, without fighting back? As a path to change, what role does taking up arms have? Where is the line between defense and offense? It is rarely, if ever, framed this way in elite-owned media, but any and all armed response to US military aggression could properly be understood as self-defense. Liberation Theology is one body of thought that explores rationales for defense against aggressors.

There are many game scenarios in which collective action is a better strategy than isolated actions. In some cases it is the opposite. Using military analogies, the phenomenon of a charge is better than one vulnerable soldier going forth at a time, while the circumstances of guerrilla warfare can give the advantage to independent and surprise acts. Social change actions would have their counterparts as, for example, with too many people at a sit-in to even try to arrest them, or a public figure being asked the same question by a different person everywhere they go.

Freedoms

Whether in the window of opportunity after a revolution or in an era of reforms, the most central question societies face when planning for themselves is "What freedoms should be chosen and codified as parameters for living in that society?" This is yet one more question for which there is no objective answer. It depends on who you ask. We have already commented that the "law of the jungle" is no law at all. A collective agreement to have bounds on behavior could, by contrast, be compared to a zoo, where no one gets to devour whomever they want and all feel safe that neither will they be devoured. This concept is canonized in what is called the social contract, credited to, among others, Jean-Jacques Rousseau in his book by that title (1762). The idea is that for a social unit like a nation to function, there is a need for all citizens to trade certain liberties for certain benefits. "Which liberties?" and "what benefits?" become the essential questions to decide.

One way to evaluate the range of kinds of liberty or freedom is by whether they enable inequality or whether they enforce or foster equality. If a relative equality is the goal, what liberties or laws would support that? What trade-offs would citizens need to agree upon to create and maintain it? The most famous formulation of how freedoms should be devised in society is the proposition by social theorist John Rawls that "Each person is to have an equal right to the most extensive basic liberty compatible with similar liberty for others." An interesting design challenge, and a good target for society, is to find the least number of laws that can uphold this or a similar chosen standard.

A cornerstone of socialism—and one reason it has been so vociferously demonized—is that there is generally no freedom to make as much money as you want. People can cry "foul" and say that a society is not free with such a constraint. But over the years, many well-informed millions (billions?) have chosen—and may yet choose—this feature as part of a contract that is favorable for themselves. A freedom to become very wealthy risks being incompatible with many other freedoms. If the wealthy run the show—as in a plutocracy—then one freedom you do not have is the right to a level playing field. Yet the hard work, gifts, and talents we so readily admire in people are a part of what lead certain individuals to gain great wealth. So what role should merit have in a sound social design? One simple guidepost is that any wealth that is earned ethically would be viewed as fair and allowed. This rule might have the interesting outcome that the most wealth-based power in society was held by principled

people—a concentration that would be either innocuous or beneficial, and was not the threat it could otherwise be.

Capitalism is often singled out as the system that enables or rewards exploitation and greed. Why, then, have socialisms sometimes
been associated with these same qualities? The answer is that it is
the specific laws or rules undergirding a society that determine if
concentrated power can infiltrate and thereby corrupt it. All govern-
mental systems have this potential vulnerability. Socialism can succumb to it. Capitalism, on the other hand, may be able to be tamed
with the right rules—though those new rules might mean it would
warrant a different name.

If too few people, owning too much, sow the seeds of societal
decline, then defining what can and cannot be owned—and what is
and is not owned initially—is important to establish. Which things
should be on record as belonging to everyone? Which things, in contrast, can be allowed to be privately owned? Resources like oil, trees,
fresh water, natural wonders, seed varieties, or the spectrum of elec-
tromagnetic wavelengths for broadcast all have been debated for in-
clusion in what we call the commons. Historically, even the "means
of production" have at times been held commonly. A progressing
concentration of power and wealth in a society usually involves pressure to privatize more and more of the commons. Since our government in the US has largely been captured by elites, national holdings
that are supposed to be our joint heritage are being lost or are being
sold from us below a market rate. Forests, aquifers, minerals, and wild
lands are just a few of the resources that the public is losing its right-
ful share of, or stake in. Less tangible things like a clean, healthful
environment, biodiversity in natural ecosystems, and forms of beauty
can also be labeled as a common heritage, and be forfeited when laws
allow their destruction.

A lawful society

Humans have a keen sense of justice. In our evolutionary past, gaining or losing in social interactions would have had a strong influence on reproductive fitness, providing the selection pressure to refine an instinct for fair accounting and help prevent us from being taken advantage of. This intuitive sense of scorekeeping runs so deep in us that it is prudent to work *with* it and avoid frustrating it when making decisions for society. If our laws and declared rights reflect this, we will have smoother sailing than if they do not.

Because of our ancestors' million-plus years of tribal living, we are probably wired to respond more to versions of peer pressure than we are to actual laws. How we are regarded by our fellow community members is of the utmost importance to most of us, and social approbation is often worth more than monetary or material gain. This is grounds for encouragement. It expands the range of possibilities for creating and maintaining civil behavior in society. With a corrupted government, fashioning laws is not a tool that the public has much access to. Alternative approaches could include a panoply of non-law means for influencing behavior, both instead of and supplemental to, lawmaking.

What are called "social dilemmas" are a category of societal problems that focus on how motives for private gain can undermine the general welfare. Without being called as much, this is a main theme of this book. Ending up either with the long or the short end of the stick in a social dilemma has everything to do with the distribution of power and who gets to make, break, or enforce the rules. Against the wishes of those who would like to have fewer rules for themselves, civilized society is the struggle to make laws or rules that can or will be followed.

Costs/benefits/incentives

A spare way of picturing social change is that we are trying to alter the cost-benefit profile of various actions. Our psychology makes the assessment of value, finding either incentives or disincentives in the available choices around us. Continuing to use our described subjective point of view for what is good and bad, favorable change can result from:

> An increase in the costs of socially negative action;
> a decrease in the benefits of socially negative action;
> an increase in the benefits of socially positive action, or;
> a decrease in the costs of socially positive action.

It is axiomatic that a change in payoffs changes the subsequent outcomes in society.

A broad social change goal could be to create the environment in which people find socially favorable choices to be more desirable than the alternatives. The current problem is simple: Under many circumstances more money can be made (or more well-being can be achieved) doing the wrong thing than by doing the right thing. This drives people—investors, CEOs, consumers, politicians—to act such that injustice, pollution, exploitation, or graft become commonplace. The challenge is to create an environment in which the right things are rewarded and can therefore flourish.

One conception of the function of government is that it has a major potential role in adjusting costs and benefits of business and consumer choices in order to better steer the course of society. A shift toward safe, clean, and sustainable energy sources is a familiar example of what a government could choose to orchestrate. Renewable energy can mean more costs for consumers and less profit for entrepreneurs—prompting neither of them to support it. Unless and until the magic number is reached wherein the return on investment in sustainable power inches above that of fossil fuels—or the cost to consumers inches below—then that road will not be taken. This can all be changed by a wide range of government tools for adjusting price. Let it be a given that government can achieve almost any social goal it sets its sights on. Our problem is that this apparatus is working primarily for the private sector and not in response to democratically decided objectives.

Beyond changing incentives like price (or return), changing the *perception* of what looks to us like a cost or a benefit is, of course, of equal importance in attempting to alter the behavior of fellow citizens. Government can certainly play a role in this approach as well, which in the US it currently does with, for example, PSAs (public service announcements) or consumer warnings. Our government also does this regularly with activities that could be classed as propaganda, including the promotional campaigns of all the branches of the military.

We are used to using the term "incentive" casually, but it turns out that there are important differences between our personal, internal reasons for doing things, and the application of external rewards for compelling actions. Many things that we choose to do, we do because the act is its own reward. And there are other things we will only do if we receive some form of compensation. A remarkable revelation psychologists have stumbled on, is that offering material incentives for things we would otherwise do of our own accord (serving meals at a soup kitchen is a suitable example to picture) disrupts our internal valuing, and can backfire as a tool for creating motivation—leading in some cases to the opposite of an intended result. What is more, the disruption of our valuing can have lasting effects, as if creating a new precedent for how society itself values something. This is referred to as the "crowding out" of personal motives by external incentives. The implications of this feature of our psychology for society are large, subtle, and complex, all at the same time. One clear take-home message is that we should honor personal motives and give them the room they need to find their full expression.

Cooperation/sharing burdens

If the US *did* choose to pursue a more costly policy of safe, clean, and sustainable energy, it could put itself at a disadvantage vis-a-vis other countries. As mentioned earlier, when two or more groups are in competition, if one of them unilaterally uses restraint or accepts more costs, it will be outdone by the other(s). Through the logic of this bind, humans are sometimes compelled to engage in socially deleterious behavior because someone else is already doing so, or would do so. Despoiling the environment, as one example, becomes almost required in order to stay apace of other companies or economies that are doing the same. In theory, if both or all parties would agree to the same restraints, no one could claim the competitive edge from such practices. Rephrased, the problem of being put at a disadvantage by doing the right thing can be resolved by getting *everyone* to do the right thing. For this to happen, there has to be enough incentive to come to the bargaining table in the first place. Many game theory games show a pattern where the highest payoff is for successful cheating (or exploitation), the second highest is for cooperation on agreeing not to cheat, and the lowest is for being cheated. This payoff matrix is intuitive and could be seen to speak volumes about our human predicaments. One trick is to lower the payoff for cheating (e.g. despoiling the environment) to the point where cooperation is what is favored instead. It is up to the public, ultimately, to create these conditions.

The idea of negotiating mutual restraint is much like a social contract—trading certain freedoms for certain benefits. As a tool for social change, cooperation on restraints has great potential. Besides trying to create the conditions where negotiating is favorable, when it *is* favorable, the opportunity should not be missed. Skills in diplomacy and mediation can be further taught and fostered. The incentive to participate in and abide by an agreement increases with both transparency and enforceability. Fear of being at a competitive disadvantage is only ameliorated if there is confidence that information about the other parties is accurate, and a collective handicap can be upheld. This is a hopeful thing about this day and age. Living a hundred years ago, I could imagine a desperate sense that there was no possibility of reining in exploitive practices because the world was simply too big, and had too little potential for accountability. Things are very different now.

Among competitors, negotiations of this sort only make sense from the top down. At a climate change summit, for instance, why would the developing world agree to reduce carbon emissions if the major powers do not? Lesser players are not likely to put themselves at a further disadvantage with unilateral restraints. A top tier, in theory, could narrow the gap between themselves and a lower tier without losing a competitive advantage. De-escalation or restraint agreements could then cascade down the line, narrowing all gaps, accordion-like.

Design considerations

The shaping of society is ultimately a bottom-up process where humans, with their different amounts of sway, contribute what they can to the larger evolving whole. But this sway can, as well, express itself in the creation of top-down guidelines to be followed by others, and which, for example in the case of a country's constitution, may endure for centuries. We have talked about the project of how to design a society—specifically one that could achieve and retain a relative social equality. Designing a society can be thought of as devising the precepts, rules, institutions, and even physical layout that become an overlay to the social and cultural environment of the citizenry. The most famous design feature of modern democracies is the system of checks and balances between branches of the US government, aimed squarely at the issue of maintaining pluralism and disbursed power. According to legal scholar Zephyr Teachout, the US Constitution, in fact, has numerous other provisions that were intended to insulate the young republic from corruption. These are described in her book, *Corruption in America: From Benjamin Franklin's Snuff Box to Citizens United*, and can be studied both for the ways they succeeded as well as failed at this goal.

There are a multitude of design ideas and social change strategies that show great potential for organizing a just society. These include ranked choice voting, democracy vouchers to fund candidates, sortition (an alternate way of selecting representatives), participatory budgeting, universal basic income, rent dividends on the use of the commons, new business ownership models, financial or monetary innovations such as reverse interest, a steeply progressive tax structure, local currencies, public banks, and a financial transaction tax—to name but a few. Conceiving a society that tries to fulfill the goals we've described quickly gets into specific proposals like these, about which there is a great abundance of material. Our focus, however, will continue to hover around the patterns and processes that organize and explain society.

With the Founding Fathers as inspiration, it is tempting to imagine embarking on the challenge of first creating and then implementing a blueprint for a good society. The reality of our situation, however, is not unlike the circumstances that urban planners face. They may long for the chance to design a beautiful, efficient, and livable city from scratch. Instead they are nearly always trying to tweak and nudge a large and complex urban system in that same direction. In society, a blank canvas happens only rarely, usually in the wake of a revolution, which introduces other complexities. Nevertheless, planning or design concepts for society may not differ greatly between working from the drawing board versus in situ—in the thick of the real life situation. The elite have been very busy designing and engineering the society that they would like. A great deal has changed, for instance, in the US in just the time frame since the beginning of the Reagan presidency. A very different design that answers to the wishes of the population at large is a project that is well underway, and that could and would have many distinctive features.

As is now familiar, positive feedback moves things, while negative feedback will stabilize something. Arguably, then, what we need is some form of positive feedback to move us to equality and negative feedback to keep us there. Natural ecosystems provide us with an elegant example of negative, or stabilizing, feedback in the shifting dynamics of plant or animal populations. We introduced this earlier as a pattern in which, when the population of an organism grows large, there will be forces that make it smaller, and when it is smaller, there will be factors that enable it to grow larger. With a range of fluctuation—like a thermostat—the organism's population size oscillates around a middle value as the numbers of its predators and prey (animal or plant) shrink and grow in their own cycles. A negative feedback or stabilizing mechanism like this for wealth or power in society is the elusive thing we are seeking. *If* motivation for greater financial security simply waned as one grew more wealthy and waxed as one grew poorer, this would lead handily to a leveling off of wealth distribution. The potlatch ceremony of the northwest coast indigenous North Americans, in which status was earned and maintained by the act of giving wealth away, is an example of a real cultural system that created this stability.

As mentioned in Chapter Two, motivation for addressing abuses of power does wax and wane and in the correct directions to create stability. Social activism and engagement in the political process increases in response to economic or related hardship, and it decreases when reforms are successful. We speculated that growth in discontent could or should, like a flywheel governor, function to keep power checked. But in recent decades such discontent has not had the magnitude necessary to succeed at this.

The counterpoint to talking about mechanisms that *stabilize* power distribution is identifying the positive feedback loops that *destabilize* an equitable society. We have touched on a dozen or more small and large loops in the preceding chapters, each of which has the outline that gains in wealth or power enable yet more wealth and power. In order to break a positive feedback loop, a value that previously cycled back to cause an effect has to not cause that effect. In a good social design, any and perhaps every positive feedback loop for power accumulation should be broken or interrupted in some way. Wealth, for example, should be prevented from being able to buy lobbying, candidates, or media domination. Of the feedback loops that can be identified, one could search out a strategy for addressing each of them. In most cases, interceding would have to do with accountability, transparency, law enforcement, regulation, internalizing of costs, or applying social pressure. These are not unfamiliar things, fortunately. They are just hard to implement against the wishes of those whose behavior they would constrain. Frustratingly, even one overlooked loop could give someone the power to undermine guards against other loops, so a sound system would need to be comprehensive.

As a general principle, arrangements where there are no conflicts of interest make for good design. Foxes can't be allowed to guard the henhouse, for instance. Modern breaches of this obvious construct include the privatization of prisons and of military functions, wherein corporations can lobby for laws and expenditures that boost their business with implications for the welfare and fate of many other parties. The public/private "revolving door," in which the motives of government employees and other public servants are tainted by opportunities for financial gain in the private sector, has become notorious in this way.

Another stabilizing concept borrowed from the natural sciences is buffering. This describes how small changes or fluctuations in a system are absorbed, or muted, preventing what might be unwanted larger-scale change. Buffering itself can be compared to the idea of inertia. When something has great inertia, small buffeting does not disrupt it or alter its course. In designing a society, it is interesting to ask how sensitive or responsive it should ideally be. How much inertia, or resistance to change, should it have? How easy, for example, should it be to change a constitution? Though an untouchable constitution is probably not the answer, if it is too easy to change, then normal fluctuations in power could allow a faction to break into the "box of rules," dooming a republic.

Malcolm Gladwell, in his book *The Tipping Point: How Little Things Can Make a Big Difference*, talks about studies that reveal the number 150 as a sort of magic size for human groupings. This is approximately the size, one theory goes, where it is possible to know everyone well enough that what they think matters. Our tribal past, on an evolutionary time scale, would be the source for this predisposition and should be taken seriously as a guide to aspects of our psychology. It is well-known that size or scale can have a profound effect on the behavior of a system. There are dozens of variables we could adjust to see how a social system reacts, but merely changing the size is among the simplest to try. Back to urban planning: As a social tool it may be that recreating tribe-sized mini-communities can play a role in helping us to feel like our original selves and to flourish socially. This resembles the idea of re-localization. Instead of the proverbial thousand-mile salad or the shirt that stopped in five countries before arriving on the rack in your nearby store, we can choose to shrink the area from which our needs are met. A diverse local or regional economy may pay many kinds of social dividends. As described in *The Economics of Happiness: Building Genuine Wealth* by Mark Anielski, greater well-being itself is an outcome of a more localized and interdependent economic and social sphere. When causes and their effects are separated by too much time or distance, it hampers accountability. Sourcing most of one's needs from a limited area narrows such gaps, enhancing transparency and the quality of information that we base our decisions on.

Effective laws, policing, and courts is one way to picture the apparatus for the maintenance of civil behavior in society. But non-law-enforcement means should certainly be superior if they work. It could be useful to imagine an honor-system society and to think through the challenging circumstances that would arise there. If people left the keys to their car in the ignition and their houses unlocked, what would tend to happen? Would it tempt bad behavior and guarantee theft? Or would it get everyone looking out for each other? For towns where this kind of trust is commonplace, what is their secret? Since social harmony can be destroyed by even a few unhappy individuals, it is smart to insure that the fabric of a community is strong, and does not have holes in it where people can, metaphorically, fall through. A prime motivator that mediates much of our behavior is the wish to be held in good stead by people we respect. Being an individual who has earned or is worthy of respect thus aligns others behind us.

It is interesting to wonder exactly what the underlying motivations are for people who devote themselves to amassing wealth. Besides security, motives could relate to pride, status, or simply besting one's peers. Perhaps there are other ways for people to fulfill the same drives. In some cases, such individuals may be the first to acknowledge that they do what they do for the challenge. If so, there may be creative ways those challenges could be retained without the fallout associated with certain personal and business practices. There are plenty of competitive arenas in society in which things are intentionally made more sporting by adjusting for various advantages, so that contestants are on an equal footing. In yacht racing, boats are given handicaps to ensure that it is skill, and not technology, that is being measured. Golf and horse racing have their counterparts.

Hunters may use just bows for an added challenge. And why would a person have "one hand tied behind their back" if not for some good sporting reason? A version of a handicap system in society to keep the playing field level could make sense. There would be many ways to go about this. A familiar one with a somewhat tarnished reputation is affirmative action. Two general choices would be to either handicap the strong players or to strengthen the weaker ones. Using good psychology in designing such a system would be paramount. Just like the hyperacuity for fairness that siblings exhibit, there may have to be some clever schemes along the lines of "you slice, and I get first pick" to insure that everyone is satisfied.

Toward a similar end, a historic precedent with a long pedigree is the Jubilee year of forgiveness, restoration, or emancipation. Whether at ten, twenty-five, or the fifty-year interval, this practice serves as a cultural reset button. Wealth could be equalized in a Jubilee year with the acknowledgment that it would then begin to concentrate all over again.

Positive feedback, you will recall, can also happen in a negative direction: the less you have, the less you can get, the less you then have. This downward spiraling is another expression of the wealth and power imbalance pattern, and part of the explanation for poverty. It is easy to solve poverty by intervening in this cycle. Solutions can involve taking power away from those who have gained an excessive share of it, or for that power to be given away voluntarily. A scholarly recognition of scenarios in which equality gravitates toward inequality in a society could play a pivotal role in laying the psychological groundwork wealthy and powerful people would naturally need before cooperating in redistribution or Jubilee-type plans.

Inherited wealth gives heirs the "initial conditions" that could lead, over generations, to extreme wealth and power. If or when this pattern is deemed to be threatening to fairness in society, then inheritance taxes can serve a role similar to the Jubilee reset, but between each generation.

There are numerous small-scale patterns in society that have a bearing on the success or failure of a governing system. The taxes that the wealthy are required to pay (theoretically more than the less wealthy) may lead them to feel they have the right to dominate politics. There is a dynamic here: Legislating to have the wealthy pay more may make them into disruptive citizens, while not having them pay more may mean they have enough of a power advantage to interfere with the functioning of a democracy.

As social animals, feedback from our peer or social groups counts for a lot. When peers influence us to influence other peers, this adds a layer that studies indicate can factor significantly into behavior choices. For example, peer pressure can be applied to show disapproval of someone who does not show disapproval of people who are acting irresponsibly. We may, to an extent, believe or expect that enforcing social behavior should be a team effort, and we keep an eye on whether others are doing their part. Game theorist Robert Axelrod refers to this level of interaction as meta-norms, and in computer models has found that "meta-norms can promote and sustain cooperation in a population." This also resembles the way that reviewers on websites can, themselves, be reviewed to reveal how many people found their comments to be useful or not. Systems that intentionally add layers of feedback or oversight may be able to steer us into new directions in society or improve accountability in certain areas. Social or peer pressures operate via subtle rules, but whether it is "keeping up with the Joneses" or "when in Rome . . . ," they are a primary way that we network our wishes and opinions with each other.

Education

Education to refine our understanding of the world is, and deserves to be, the perennial focus of efforts to improve society. The more we learn, and the more accurate that learned information is, the better citizens we can be, and the less we are subject to demagoguery and to being misled. There is scarcely an academic discipline the knowledge from which does not somehow bear on the potential quality of that citizenship. The study of history, economics, psychology, biology, physics, and others can equip us to spot fallacious arguments when we encounter them, and to formulate correct views on matters in the world around us. A well-educated population is among the most significant stabilizing features of a society, acting as a buffer and enabling it to self-correct when disrupted.

Educating against the current of elite (including commercial) self-interested persuasion is not a simple thing. Similar to the paradox of the Big Lie that we mentioned in Chapter Two, the more a truth diverges from what someone already believes, the harder it is to teach that truth. Should a watered down-truth or a half-truth be used and taught at times instead as a stepping stone to full truth? One could certainly lose credibility—and with it one's audience— by discussing the most extreme transgressions coming from elite quarters. But an abridged version of the facts could be detected as just that and fail to be compelling. Increasing the believability of truth by presenting the background that makes it make sense is a sensible approach.

Ethical criteria

Somewhere along the line, the two-word phrase "politically correct," or "political correctness," entered our lexicon. As it has worked out, the term is almost always used as a negative retort against the advocate for "correct" views or behavior. In more innocent times (the '70s, if I recall) it was the equivalent of a mild rebuke to someone for giving out a little too much free advice about what they thought was the right way to act. Later, the term transitioned to become a reply to rigid or suffocating rules for speech and for thinking. Along the way it has also taken an Orwellian turn whereby the person using the quip is sometimes the one being more authoritarian than the correctness they are supposedly challenging. To the point, however: In several of its uses the phrase tends to put the kibosh on what may be sincere efforts to encourage more attention to ethical concerns. I think we should be careful not to allow potentially laudable ideas for how we act with one another to be conflated with dictating or regimenting behavior. A middle ground certainly exists. Above and beyond this tangle of intents, some means of popularizing and reinforcing ethical behavior could reorient decision-making throughout society, making it admirable to look for, and spell out, underlying ethical considerations in business practices, or in purchasing and investment choices, for example.

In public life in the US at this time, moral considerations are not a primary criterion for deciding things and generally take a back seat to both economic concerns—such as jobs or growth—and to the nearly catch-all category of national security. Currently, the President, and other public officials, cannot say anything that could potentially damage the standing or profitability of a prominent business or industry. This is a huge constraint, since anyone without that effective gag order could easily come up with statements to inspire genuinely constructive directions for society. Almost any proposal suggesting less use of resources or less consumption runs this risk of offending an interest group. Civic leaders, as well as scholars, should be able to speak freely from a moral stance. Rather than this being considered irresponsible if it disturbed the revenue of specific businesses, it could be seen as a guidepost for consumers and producers alike, and set precedents that inform other activities in society. If we were, for example, to propose to rethink the inhumane treatment of animals in the industrial agriculture sector, we would have to simultaneously talk openly about the self-interested social forces that would oppose the idea. Such connections need to be aired candidly. An attitude that it is tough luck if someone invested in an industry that was destined to go the way of the dinosaurs may be necessary at times. Ethical, as well as other prudent or precautionary criteria, could be elevated to their appropriate place in what would then be a saner society.

Interpersonal psychology

The field of psychology is regularly coming up with eye-opening insights into what really makes us tick. Cleverly designed experiments can show us things about our tendencies toward kindness or unkindness, mechanisms of self-justification, our relationship to authority, or the details of our allegiance to social groups. Anything to do with psychology has also to do with the origin of our cultural circumstances and how we may act in response to them.

Among the most significant and deeply seated of our emotions are the ones that can emerge, full blown, in a matter of seconds. Jealousy is one of these. Reacting to certain injustices may be another. For most of us there is something stirring in brushing up against simple caring and kindness. Some stories bring almost immediate tears to our eyes. Someone humbly showing their vulnerability can be both disarming and bonding. What is behind these experiences? That such wiring—and such a reservoir of emotion—should exist in us may hint at a great potential source for transformation in individuals and, hence, society.

Engaging in what we might call "ego-maintenance behavior" (a self-descriptive term) can elicit ego-maintenance behavior from others in response. There is positive feedback in this kind of guarded manner, which, like one-upmanship, can lead to a defensive standoff between individuals. Positive feedback can happen in the opposite direction as well, with personal disclosure and a generous attitude catalyzing the same or similar in return. Some form of positive feedback, as we mentioned, would be ideal for expediting society to a new and favorable attractor. If generosity breeds generosity, then what are we waiting for?

A person's receptivity to changing their behavior may be influenced by our attitude about them. For individuals such as politicians, business leaders, or other public figures, the option of reversing course on a stance can be aided by helping them retain their pride and stature. Whether in personal matters or in public life, one of the more generous, and also constructive, things we can do is to support a person's ego. Losing face is the hardest and most unlikely way that people make change. If we are praised for, or feel proud of, a new stance or belief, then it is an easy transition. Our behavior and attitude create the "space" in which people can act differently.

Only genuine respect has the quality of initiating receptivity and openness in others. This has been taught by many both religious and secular teachers and traditions. Nonviolent Communication, or NVC, is one well-known model for this disposition. Ram Dass, an influential voice to the baby-boom generation, spoke of not putting people "out of your heart." Respecting all, Jesus and others have taught, means including the "least among you," and your enemies—i.e. everyone. Nonviolent philosophy emphasizes that pacifism does not mean passive and that we must teach people how we want to be treated. There would be, thus, an art to challenging and confronting—but not forsaking—the elite on certain of their actions. An empowering idea is that some elites and their collaborators may want to be stopped. If so, and in the spirit of an "intervention," we must do them the kindness of stopping them.

Complexity can emerge in a self-organizing system even when the active agents in the system operate by very simple rules. In the case of society, humans operate by not-so-simple rules, and this only enlarges the scope of possibilities for what can unfold as we interact. Group experiences, in particular, represent a treasure trove for discovering the breadth of what we are capable of together. A planned process for a group could be for the goal of making a collective decision, designing something (this is sometimes called a charrette), resolving a conflict, or simply creating good feelings or a "high" among the participants. There are what can be thought of as technologies for effecting these and other outcomes in groups: following a reproducible outline or formula in order to achieve a given result. The ability of a group to make decisions with the greatest amount of satisfaction among its members is particularly important in culture. The role of a facilitator is one thing that can be priceless in this regard. Many experiments have been done exploring how to achieve consensus or unanimity in groups. Developing knowledge and skill in this area gets right to the heart of the spirit of democracy and of a society based on broad participation.

Because of the psychological phenomenon of self-justification, if you can get a person to do something once, they are more likely to rationalize it as a good thing than if they had not taken that step. Similarly, an investment of money or time in one direction means there can be internal discord if a different choice is then made. A financial donation to a cause, signing of a petition, attending a new kind of event, or buying clothing of a certain style means we are then slightly predisposed to defend those things and to act in accord with that choice in the future. This self-justification tendency can be used to initiate new directions in others by getting people to take the first step, suggesting a pathway to changing points of view in society— albeit one that has long been recognized and utilized in marketing.

Daily interactions that involve our family life, office life, driving experiences, and more are packed with possibilities for varied outcomes and for insight into our "wiring." These settings can provide grist for thought experiments that suggest solutions to larger-scale matters. The proverbial schoolyard fight, for example, mirrors certain societal themes. One of these is the difficulty of trying to exit from an altercation with pride intact. If two entangled combatants are pulled apart by their respective comrades, both have the blessing of appearing as if they *could* have won, and are then better able to put the incident behind them. Vicious cycles of trying to "even the score" are notoriously hard to resolve and are better averted if possible. Some patterns in society may be fractal in nature and have essentially the same dynamic on different scales.

A deeper understanding of our psychology, informed by evolutionary theory, can—besides shedding continuing light on human culture—give further clues to sound social change strategies. This may be what elites have long been doing to gain cooperation and capitulation: putting sophisticated psychological insights into practice across the spectrum of cultural channels.

Two drawbacks of equality

If a relative equality of wealth and power were to become widespread on Earth, then humanity would have at least two new, interrelated challenges. Without poverty, an equal resource consumption per person could turn out to be either unsustainable for the planet or unacceptably low for individuals. There are people who crunch numbers for things just like this, and the word is that we are already living beyond the ability of Earth's resources and natural services to support us—and that is with one third of the seven-and-a-half-billion-person population having an ecological footprint of close to zero. Such realities should be the signal that the developed world will need to learn to live with less, and the developing world can no longer aspire to that same profligate model. Practices associated with conquest—or protection from conquest—may currently account for a majority of resource use and environmental degradation on the planet. This is the good news, since a future without military conflict is easy to visualize. The issue of who is entitled to use how much resource is a major one to solve, and gets back to questions of rights and freedoms, only this time on the scale of the whole planet.

Differences of opinion

We have all but avoided talking about specific alternative schools of thought for how to structure a government—including whether it should be representative government or one without representatives, that utilized direct democracy. Some of the names that alternatives go by are distributism, communalism, individualism, libertarianism, socialism, and anarchism. Capitalism and democracy, themselves, have variants, including social democracy. Two important variables, which are often debated, are how large government should be and to what extent should we engage in collective undertakings like pooling money for common benefit. People vary widely in their views and opinions on choices such as these. Receptivity to arrangements in which taxes are high and government provides commensurate services may depend mostly on cultural precedent, or the proof of a familiar well-functioning example. If government is corrupted, then large is arguably worse than small, because large would have more opportunities to redistribute wealth upward. But if a government is fair and democratic, then large could easily offer a net gain to the population. If there is no obvious better version—large fair government vs. small fair government—this may be a hard philosophical point to settle. The subject is a worthy and interesting chance to publicly discuss the finer points of what best governance would look like.

Majority problem

A relative equality of influence may sound like the best goal we can name for society, but there are a series of subtle problems that can be associated even with the celebrated majority rule. What if, for instance, the majority decided to invade an unthreatening country? Or to have slaves? Or, once, to cut down all the trees on—and seal the fate of—Easter Island? In the US we appear to vote for unsustainable environmental practices and a belligerent foreign policy. But, you say, we are more of a plutocracy than a democracy, and therefore not true majority rule. What, though, if we were a healthy democracy and yet voted for those policies? Decisions made fairly by a majority of a population are not automatically sacrosanct. There is a strong case for obeying the laws of the land when they are arrived at democratically. There is, however, also a strong case for acting based on a moral code, following the voice of our conscience, even when it is contrary to the voice of the majority. This seems to be an inescapable corollary to the value and virtue of working within a group process.

A majority vote may also threaten the interests of a minority. This is what elites have to fear—and historically they have. That fear may help propel the accumulation of power, since elites know there could be consequences, possibly including prosecutions, if the power of the majority were to increase. In Occupy Wall Street parlance, the 99 percent could level the playing field to the detriment of the 1 percent. Wealth or assets could be nationalized, or debt declared odious. This threat may have been particularly pronounced in Revolutionary-era America since every household owned a gun, and wealth had not yet built up institutional bulwarks to insulate itself. The argument must have been common that aristocrats could not risk a one-person-one-vote governing system for all they might stand to lose.

A politician who promises to redistribute unequal wealth should, in theory, be able to win. But for a range of reasons they currently do not tend to. Because the populace outnumbers the elite, there is power and leverage waiting to be used in countless constructive ways. The problem identified variously as a "tyranny of the majority," "democratic despotism" or "majority faction," may or may not pose much of a threat. A majority will usually have more incentive to level the playing field than to make it un-level in their favor. When a majority responds in order to constrain exploitive or autocratic actions of a minority, this is appropriate, or to be expected. An abusive majority, when it exists, is likely to be the product of manipulation by a *minority* interest, which should be addressed as a different kind of problem.

One criticism of democracy is that it is like two wolves and a sheep voting on what to have for dinner, to which I ask, "What is the alternative—should the two wolves and the sheep write a constitution together to codify protections?" It has also been said that a republic secures our liberties, where a democracy leaves them open to be voted away. But, first of all, *no* liberty is secure, and secondly, *some* mode of decision-making is needed to work out ongoing details of how to arbitrate our getting along. The writing of the US Constitution was clearly the product of a compromise, where factions influenced it in proportion to their power at the time. A constitution written today or at any future time would reflect this same reality. The distribution of influence and sway is the all-important factor in matters of governance.

Challenges of redistribution

If a fair society is to be achieved and maintained, power will have to be redistributed. It is an interesting question, though, whether or not wealth also needs to be redistributed. The reason that we have been roughly equating wealth with power as forces in society is because wealth is a means for manifesting things, which hearkens back to our definition of power as a measure of one's ability to affect and to influence their environment. In the wake of a social transformation it is possible to limit the ways that wealth can translate into power by, for instance, constraining its use in the political sphere. This said, there are a number of good arguments for attempting to redistribute certain wealth. As would be the case in normal judicial proceedings, if money is gained through criminal activity, this warrants restitution. (If wealth is gained legally according to laws that were written by people who had abused their power and the public trust, then this is a larger question.) A day may come when complex judgments will need to be made to determine whose wealth was earned fairly and whose was not.

This reasoning applies to illegitimate debt as well. (Debt, and being indentured to another, could be thought of as a sort of negative power, or power deficit, and an obstacle to manifesting things.) Much debt of the developing world, for instance, is clearly the product of corrupt machinations from high places. There is a further argument that the US owes reparations to the countries it has unjustly invaded or meddled with. Most of these violations have been public enough that the fact of them not being actively challenged by the US populace means that not just elite plotters, but all US citizens, should pay toward reparations. We are talking about redistributing power in order to create a fair society and a fair world going forward, so it is as important that this happen between an imperial power and its targeted countries as it is within the US itself.

How many years back in time should such settlements cover? That presents an awkward question as well, since whoever fell just before any cutoff date could rightly feel aggrieved. A similar circumstance would apply to other kinds of recompense, like canceling or reducing student loan debt, as well as to things like making higher education free. A phasing in, or out, is one idea for maintaining good will. There would be others.

International

In order to simplify some arguments, it has been useful to talk mostly about affairs within the United States. However, much of the ground we are surveying needs some degree of translation to a supranational version, which is, increasingly, the world we inhabit. Elites segregate into factions, but these factions are not synonymous with countries. With globalization, a law in one country may just chase a corporation to another country. Elites either create fertile ground where they are, or they go elsewhere to find it. Their interests are complex, but similar enough that they regularly convene in global gatherings. There may be a discernible nation-based hierarchy of who controls whom—or there may not be. Social justice movements can also be transnational or supranational and are frequently ideologically aligned with each other, if not actually allied.

A comprehensive set of strategies to prevent, slow down, or reverse a concentration and abuse of power would ultimately have to be global in its scope. Curtailing the dominance of one country by implementing a more effective rule by the people could very well leave a less constrained superpower or elite faction to gain in response. If the US, for instance, were to be weakened geopolitically by citizen demands within the country, would this then allow a no-holds-barred competitor to end up reigning over a future world government instead? The meta level to contests is that strategies, and even conversations or contemplations about strategies, often have to be hidden to be effective. This applies to things ranging from mating to business plans to global politics. So if, for example, the US-based elite knew that the China-based elite had authoritarian plans for the world, and they were trying to foil this—even on our behalf—they could not necessarily tell us. How should this once-removed level of thinking be factored in by citizens of nations? For one, like the boy in the "Emperor's New Clothes" story, it should probably be blurted out. Open discussion and disclosure is almost always salutary and has a potential to lead to breakthroughs. Social action coordination with foreign populations may be necessary and increasingly workable in the years ahead—each, for example, demanding the same concessions from their governments.

One thing that global candor should or could clarify is why, exactly, does the current extension of the arms race rage on between at least China, Russia, and the West? The gargantuan expenditures as well as human and ecological costs of this drama—including the weaponization of space—is the single greatest curse on the planet.

The first question that has to be answered about the contest is who, if anyone, is acting offensively to raise the ante, and who is responding defensively to keep up. What if everybody thinks they are just being defensive—almost a misunderstanding on an apocalyptic scale? The most hopeful situation would be "If they will stop, I will stop, too." A well-publicized global invitation to disarm with assurances should be able to expose any country's true motives, and whether or not they are the ones propelling the competition: in effect, calling somebody's bluff. Quite seriously, it could even be that the whole racket is so lucrative just as an end in itself, that the players (even unconsciously) look for ways to keep it going.

Differences in national character are often striking, when looking around the globe. One component of these differences is the degree of independence of thought in a country's citizens. Television hours-per-person-per-day is one kind of metric that can help explain this particular variation. US citizens lead in this world statistic, with an average of close to four hours of TV viewing each day. Whether there is, or is not, a cause and effect here, most of the discouraging news we have surveyed in these chapters is about US citizens and their inattentiveness to corruption. It could very well be that people of other nations can and will be the ones to bring us here in the US to our senses, stop us as we deserve to be stopped, and take the lead in charting out the better future. As we have mentioned, enculturation (the teaching and learning of culture) and socialization have their own conundrum that follows reasoning similar to the power conundrum: A culture cannot be redeemed, or its virtues resurrected, if the values that this depends on have slipped below a threshold. For the US, such a decline would become a checkmate situation, where elites take the game. If the US can't save itself—because we have slipped below this threshold—then the next best hope is that the requisite values and accompanying power are intact somewhere outside of the US to do what we cannot do. Obviously, a possibility exists that the elite can checkmate the entire world.

CHAPTER FIVE

Getting There From Here

Humanity is currently way out on a limb. We are gambling with our greatest gifts and treasures: those of liberty, sound health, a vibrant natural world, and the chance to be proud of the legacy we leave to our descendants. Some of us are running roughshod over this beautiful planet, and others are letting it happen. Timeless themes of stewardship, reverence, and caring are losing out to extraction, plunder, and disregard. There are a number of absolute dead ends that we could face, and many more scenarios in which the quality of living on Earth just degrades. These trends are well chronicled. The only point to now add is that a large amount of change is needed in a short amount of time if we are to retain some of the best that life here has to offer. Urgency, blessedly, has the potential to sharpen awareness, hone our thinking, and reorder priorities and resources toward overcoming obstacles.

It is by now familiar logic that we see how a relatively few people can gain the lion's share of power in society, or that tyranny can win out over the liberty of individuals in a country or in the entire world. But the behavior of social systems remains hard to fully understand or predict. Culture has its wild cards, and system behaviors are replete with thresholds and tipping points. On one hand, the complexity of our societies can tempt us to surrender to forces and dynamics that seem to be beyond our control. But the same complexity reveals that there is no room for fatalism or resignation. We *do* have control of the force we each individually exert on the cultural landscape around us. And when creativity and passion are harnessed to reason in the form of analysis or strategizing, our role in the complex interplay of society can be incisive and profound.

We have built the case that the inventory of threats to our well-being which any of us can name, originate, in many instances, with self-interested gains being made by disproportionately powerful individuals. To the extent to which this is true, the collective exigencies of our time trace to a source that is specific enough to be the kernel of a game plan. If this is right, and with a little luck, then an all-out effort to rectify inequalities of power could banish a large portion of our superficially far-flung problems.

There is near-consensus worldwide on the Golden Rule or its equivalent. This means that the whole world has something very basic and important in common. This is the world's "common law" in a sense. We have described it as "not harming others, and acting with the greater good in mind," but there are many ways to say this that capture its spirit. Referencing this is like going back to first principles in the sciences. In society, statutory laws are built stepwise on top of what feels to the majority of humans like the right foundational principles. This, again, is the essence of a bottom-up process that leads to top-down practices. Except to the extent to which enculturation can alter or erase values and yearnings, this common law is the kind of law that can't be rewritten by elites to suit themselves. With power in the right hands, it is reassuring to believe there may be very little disagreement on what the nature of justice and fairness would look like. It is important to observe that for this Golden Rule ethic as our common law, elite behavior is almost entirely outside the law—which serves to highlight the fact that new laws, written by the public, would be very different from those of the present.

It is heartening that empirical studies continue to strengthen the observation that humans are very interested in cooperating with each other, and that we promote and encourage this in our acts of generosity and kindness. Further, the motives or mechanisms for this instinct seem to extend well beyond the benefits accrued by either helping relatives (kin altruism) or taking part in reciprocal exchanges. Instead, there appears to be what is termed a "group selection" explanation, where altruism benefits the tribe or group, which then is more likely to survive—with you, the altruist, within it. Samuel Bowles and Herbert Gintis, both of the Santa Fe Institute, cover these developments in detail in their book *A Cooperative Species: Human Reciprocity and Its Evolution.* There is nothing here to shake a stick at! We are wired for the best, and the trick will be to find ways to bring this out. But I do not think that this particular cluster of virtues can, alone, save the day. It is what would be called "necessary, but not sufficient." Among the traits most confounding to our search for planetary harmony are that we appear to be easily fooled, and easily taken advantage of—plus, a surprising number of people have a soul that they seem to be willing to sell.

The crux

A headlong effort to first understand and then vocally address the corrupting of the world's compromised democracies is a focus of the game plan I referred to above. But the puzzle we face, at least in the US, is that we have all but painted ourselves into a corner, and the path out from that corner is neither obvious nor easy. Years of waning power have left the population with fewer choices and many constraints. We are in the dicey position of not currently having much clout, leverage, or sway, and needing to come up with ways to gain more of each. Whatever strategy or approach is used to effect social change, it has to begin with the reality of the present. We begin where we *can* begin. In a good business plan one uses whatever money they start with to try to make more money, getting the business to grow the business. The power that resides in the populace needs to be grown in the same manner: in an iterating cycle, using existing power to create more power. If this feels familiar, that is because it is the same positive feedback that built the elite themselves into the sizable force they are today. Starting with less does not change the dynamic. What is key, however, is that—since power distribution is zero-sum—the power of the citizenry needs to grow *relative* to that of the elite, in order for gains to be real.

Narrowed choices

Today, open avenues for effecting social change are fewer than they were a decade ago, and fewer still than a decade before that. If once you could use your dollars to support a locally-owned stationery store, that chance is gone when there are only large corporate counterparts to choose from. If once a person could confidently go to the press or the authorities about illegal or improper actions they have witnessed, a chill sets in when whistleblowers themselves are prosecuted and convicted in record numbers. When a voter feels they are chronically stuck choosing between the lesser of two evils, it means their real vote cannot be cast, and voice cannot be heard. While some single billionaire individuals offer an effective expense account to their chosen cause or candidate, other efforts rely on scarcely allocated $20 donations. With NSA infringements on privacy or with the passage of the 2007 NDAA (National Defense Authorization Act), which removes the guarantee of due process, constitutional protections are being whittled away. All of this forces greater strategic thinking. We are left to ask, "What can be done in spite of, or in the face of, the reality of concentrated power?" One reply to this question is to commence growing a countering power by means that are as fast and as expeditious as possible.

Expanded choices

One could suppose that the profit motive drives the direction of society. And this is true, to the extent that it is, because many of the biggest players are preoccupied with this kind of gain. But what really drives society is motivation for gain in well-being, and financial reward is just one form that this takes. How many kinds of well-being can we name? Answer: enough to suggest a variety of different approaches to redirecting the course of society. People are motivated by a wish to be affirmed and respected. They are motivated by their empathy toward others, by love of nature, love for loved ones, an appreciation of truth and reason, pride at being right, pride at being good, desires for justice, and the prestige of being accomplished. People are motivated by both a need to conform (to the right extent) and by a need to be different and distinctive (to the right extent). As citizens concerned about the world around us, we can tap into this full range of wishes and desires in order to help effect social change. Through our actions and deeds we shape the opportunities that lead to greater well-being in others. At root, our life choices alter the cultural landscape in which other people make their life choices. The trick, as we have said before, is to create an environment that brings forth constructive behavior in our fellow humans. Fashioning that environment so people will not gain by making socially detrimental choices is a part of this picture. Where we can, we pursue changes to the economic landscape or to the rules of society—influencing the price of goods, or changing laws in order to alter incentives. Other approaches supplement and complement these. Importantly, everyone still always chooses what they think will be best for them. "We" have just either changed the selection or influenced the perception of value.

Affirming good behavior is the surest way to get more of it. Life is full of chances to acknowledge or reward acts that we admire. This is particularly valuable when people have stretched a little in what they have done. On the other side of the coin, it is important to be forthright about what we consider to be unacceptable behavior. From the reflexive raising of one's eyebrows to a full-blown rebuke in the editorial column of the newspaper, messages of disapproval are integral to human communication. Whether or not it is apparent, people register disfavor and usually attempt to chart a path to reduce it. Many elite acts warrant anger and outrage. There is great power to harness in these emotions, and in strong emotions generally.

In dialogue, appealing to people's intelligence compliments them that they are smart and raises the level of discourse. Appealing to people's wisdom compliments them that they are wise. Appealing to people's kindness compliments them that they are kind, and encourages just that. This recalls the famous experiment in which students of equal ability rose or sank to the level of achievement their teachers were told to expect from them. This thinking applies to interactions with the elite as much as it does to others.

Things that catch on

Acting as individuals in our communities and in the world at large, we can teach, advocate, foster, and model. Culture is created in our wake. Up to a point, culture is the sum of the contributions of individuals. But group interactive processes also feed on each other to create trends, movements, fads, new mores, and other new cultural attributes. For a variety of reasons people will copy or emulate each other, giving any small, novel development in culture the chance to grow. As highly social animals we care a great deal what other people think of us. Things that contribute to shaping our reputation or that give us status make up the biggest wild card in culture. Practically anything can come to be associated with pride, esteem, or being hip. Who, in a million years, would have guessed that men and women, in large numbers and across many social subcultures, would now be choosing to turn their bodies into virtual illuminated manuscripts with tattoos! Surprises like this are reassuring and should pique our imaginations for how status could come to be linked with a social good.

Malcolm Gladwell describes what he calls "contagious" ideas. These are words, images, or objects that spread through the population for some unique appeal they have. Something just like this may be a key that unlocks a worldwide passion and insistence for change. Like the emergence of a new meaning for "occupy" in 2011, or the Vietnam-era "Give Peace a Chance," words and phrases can become a symbol and rallying cry in a movement. As I write, the World Freedom Alliance is gaining traction under a banner that needs no explanation and could attract any and all who are concerned about threats to democracy. In the familiar notion of a tipping point, it is positive feedback that kicks in at the "point." From there, more becomes more, and less becomes less, as a wholesale shift is set in motion. Activism can have a more-breeds-more quality, particularly among the youth who are apt to be seeking a peer group identity, and hence be searching out ideas to bond around. Heroes unite and inspire us. We can actively work to make heroes out of worthy people doing worthy things. The most efficient and productive approaches to change are capable of creating ripple, watershed, domino, self-catalyzing, multiplier, or chain reaction effects. Anything that can begin on a small scale and has an ability to spread is a good formula for social change. Ethics like leaving things better than we found them or giving more than we take might have appeal to catch on in this way. A general goal could be to get within the "gravitational field" of attractors for socially favorable alternatives, where acts for the greater good would catalyze more of the same. Identifying these attractors—where positive feedback does the rest of the "work" for you—could be an important specialty for social change planners.

A one dollar—or one cent—difference in price in a market determines when something becomes more favorable than the alternatives. As soon as this threshold is passed, entrepreneurs, investors, or consumers would logically abandon one path for another. Potential tipping points like this lurk in the marketplace, waiting to be pushed to and over the edge, including via increases in knowledge and awareness among the public.

No one wants to be on the wrong side of history. People will align behind what they think, or sense, is both correct and inevitable. We look for which way the wind is blowing and recalculate our opinions as the cultural consensus changes. A shift in a positive direction moves the center of gravity along with it, and people can then look further over the horizon from there. Some elites, as we mentioned in Chapter Two, are persuaded that rule by the few is what is inevitable, and so it is better to become one of those few, than to not. If we, on the other hand, can demonstrate the inevitability of democracy, then more people will realign their lives in anticipation of that. This implies a tipping point psychology which, in this case, means social change endeavors could strike gold if they get within reach of the impression that democracy will be a certainty, and that avenues for unethical gain will be coming to an end.

Progress in assembling a jigsaw puzzle follows positive feedback: the more the picture becomes clear, the faster it becomes even clearer. If understanding societal problems showed this same pattern, then knowledge and insight could build at an accelerating rate as the "picture" became clearer.

And then some

There are probably strategic paths that could most effectively turn power into more power. Electoral reform is a good example of a route that could lead to a cascade of new possibilities, following on a renewed confidence in both voting and serving in office. Many have commented that starting working locally, then expanding outward from there, is the best way to ultimately achieve larger scale change. If power is limited, one can adopt a strategy of influencing people who can then influence others, on up the line—a stepwise approach, reaching those within reach, who can reach those within their own reach. If citizens needed to prioritize activism, they could work from a version of the risk matrix notion mentioned earlier, choosing the most consequential or threatening themes in society as the first ones to address.

One prudent tack is to look for and make use of the best remaining serviceable infrastructure that is responsive to the public. This may include aspects of the legal system, academia, state or local government, the Freedom of Information Act, or the ballot initiative process, for example. This amounts to utilizing, and not taking for granted, avenues for change that are open and available. It is also smart to keep an eye out for "low hanging fruit," such as the ready leverage associated with a corporation's public image or the window of relative openness to candidates and the media during the presidential primary season. Power should not be squandered. As a case in point, forever being a loser in winner-take-all endeavors is not generally productive without the hope of building to be able to win. It is better to choose a winner-take-all arena in which one can win or to find a setting in which gains are measured differently.

As corruption in a society advances, it becomes increasingly hard for important disclosures to make their way into the public realm. Whistleblowers, or the equivalent, would have the goal of succeeding at sharing their information without endangering themselves. This is particularly challenging for insiders who would like to maintain their anonymity and cover. Getting information only into the hands of small or alternative news outlets may be a dead end. Intrepid journalists who can push a story into prominence are one avenue, but they have their own established reputations to factor in A general strategy would be to use a blitz, with multiple outlets and repositories for the information. Leaving the country first is an extreme choice that has its place. Often there may be just one chance to successfully make a disclosure. The easier and safer this is, the more will be forthcoming. Beyond the circumscribed needs of legitimate national security, pursuits like this help counteract power that relies on secrecy and lack of accountability.

The magnitude of any given elite crime, if and when it is exposed, is proportional to several things: The worse the crime, the stronger the outrage. The worse the crime, the more it arouses suspicion about other crimes by the same, or related, individuals. The worse the crime, the more it can result in sustained vigilance by society in the future. Following from this, the worse the crime, the more capacity its exposure may have to catalyze substantive and lasting social change. This is a reason in itself to be receptive to citizen and alternative media probes into events of the day. Proof of betrayal, in particular, arouses strong emotions that could help drive a popular challenge to elite-held power.

A single incident that precipitates a system change is an interesting kind of possibility for society, including on the world stage. Fiction writers have often worked this theme, as when the landing of extraterrestrials or the looming threat of an asteroid impact transforms the lives of all humanity, putting people in touch with higher-order needs. A commonplace example of this kind of shift would be the way the sound of a siren on a roadway abruptly restructures the cars and drivers, unifying them toward a purpose, and rendering moot any petty frustrations that might have existed the moment before. Gratitude for a single act of heroism that happened to be by someone from one country helping members of another is an example of the kind of thing that has the power to eclipse animosities, and to almost erase borders. The climax to the 1966 movie *The Russians Are Coming, The Russians Are Coming* illustrates a similar scenario when a New England boy is rescued from the heights of a church roof by an instinctual and spontaneous team effort between the locals and the Russian sailors. Transformation is the operable word in these examples.

It is virtually an axiom of a well-functioning society that there needs to be oversight, in some form, of one another's behavior. The full picture of accountability in society includes knowing, first, who did what. Then, where it applies, there is a response or consequence. At least the first of these steps has the potential to be greatly enhanced by the ongoing emergence of new electronic technologies. Even the proliferation of cameras, alone, may be on its way to radically changing the mechanics of accountability. The same could be true of hacking, with its capacity to stymie attempts at secrecy, since it is unlikely that elites can gain a monopoly on the skill that this depends on.

These days almost everything under the sun—from college professors, to eBay buyers and sellers, to Facebook posts—is being rated by others to ostensibly improve our experience of navigating a complex world. Whether or not this will feel like too much at some point, there is still a long way that it could go. Since many of our larger societal problems have to do with people cheating or deceiving us, there is clearly a need for learning who can or cannot be trusted. The means are now there to create what could be called "e-accountability." Might there be a coefficient of reliability for each of us, which, like a credit rating, can be looked up by others? Such developments are probably anathema to most of us, but it is reasonable for the public to keep an open mind on how to manage the general problem of people who would pull the wool over our eyes for one reason or another. In theory, the chance exists to create a dossier on individuals who might be keeping one on us.

Successful propaganda effectively casts a spell. It is part of the challenge to a truth-seeking public to find the right antidote, or the right incantations, to counteract or undo that spell. Better still, well-informed people will find that they are automatically inoculated against attempts to mislead. Foster Gamble, of the Thrive movement, suggests that immersion, or sustained exposure to a given perspective, is the most effective way to alter a person's views. There may be a critical saturation level at which this happens. A move away from elite viewpoints could progress naturally as alternative media sources proliferate, offering an integrated worldview from which people do not merely bounce back to their previous views. A version of sustained exposure could be pursued as an intentional education or media technique.

There are some setups in which one almost can't lose. Publishing or posting material that is revelatory and is also of unimpeachable quality means attempts to censor it can backfire, drawing more people to discover it. This would be the Streisand effect, named for that celebrity's attempt to conceal the location of her mansion, which led to a thousand-fold increase in how many people knew about it. Censoring or banning books, videos, or individuals can end up having this same result—but may take some strategic nudging to get going.

Since we have acknowledged that different sides to the same person will be brought out by different circumstances, then a quest for a good society really means working for and against certain attributes, and not for and against certain individuals. If it is the behaviors we focus on, this creates the most room for any person to change, themselves, as the world changes around them.

Plato

The tendency of governing systems to degenerate toward tyranny has been examined at some length by no less a figure than Plato—a participant in and observer of the Athenian democracy of his day. A concern of his which he highlights is that the populace, or the "masses," are not well educated or refined enough to be able to properly guide the state, and that with a democracy, this contributes to its undoing. In the US it could be argued that we are making Plato's point for him—namely, that a healthy democracy *does* depend on the right qualities among its custodians, and that the public has been failing at its role of guiding and protecting the state. This is exactly the reason why education and the cultivation of character are of the highest priority in the race to earn back control of our government. Plato mentions wisdom, reason, and experience in philosophizing as traits that would be needed. Enfolded within these qualities would be savvy about the dynamics of power and the potential for its abuse.

Instead of a democracy, Plato's ideal state is what he calls an "aristocracy," and is ruled by "philosopher kings." The idea is that rule by wise, benevolent, and incorruptible individuals is the surest formula for a successful government and society. There is a lot to be said for this concept, but it immediately raises the question of who chooses these philosopher kings. If benevolent people should run the government, then probably it would take benevolent people to choose to place them there. But where would those benevolent people necessarily get that authority? From yet other like-minded benevolent people? Whatever ideal system one chooses from the comfort of an armchair—or Greek proscenium—the next relevant question is always if, and how, it could be implemented, starting from real life circumstances.

Plato's aristocracy doesn't happen to draw its cues from the populace, but other than that, it is similar to the corruption-proof government we have been striving to conceptualize here. He says the rulers must be kept away from any corrupting influence, should therefore have restrictions, and that only people who volunteer to accept these restrictions could rule. This is similar to laws that would attempt to preserve the integrity of our legislators by forbidding gifts or bribes, and by controlling lobbying and campaign funding. One could argue, though, that if rulers or representatives were to any extent corruptible, rules constraining their behavior would eventually be eroded via the very powers granted to them.

The most comprehensive solution to the vulnerabilities inherent in governments would be to find a way to choose truly incorruptible individuals for leadership roles. Curiously, if the citizenry elected such trustworthy leaders, people would not need to ride herd on them and could devote less time to political concerns—an incentive in itself, perhaps, for ensuring this. Rules constraining the actions of leaders with this integrity would not be needed and could even be counterproductive, undermining the pride associated with the rarified role they have been given. (People who are incorruptible may not necessarily be saints to the extent that they are unconcerned about pride!) Incorruptibility is a trait that may go with humility and not go with self-promotion—so a *lack* of interest in serving may be the kind of indicator that someone would be a good candidate. The popular selection of a benevolent monarch is one version of how to organize a country around this formula. More familiar, and likely in the US, would be representative government with incorruptible representatives. This idea could be adapted to actually develop techniques or methods for finding these individuals and promoting the concept. On a list of qualifications for public office, integrity and incorruptibility deserve to be at or near the top.

Enablers/psychology

The position the elite maintain at the top of the socioeconomic pecking order is only possible with collaboration, cooperation, or acquiescence from multiple other tiers of society. Historian and author Howard Zinn, as well as others, have pointed out the Achilles heel this represents for the elite. Without police, without soldiers, without key judges and members of the media, the elite would be as turtles on their backs—powerless and vulnerable. Following the right social tipping point, Zinn imagines a "revolt of the guards" in which these legions that the elite depend on simply don't show up for work, don't keep silent, don't agree to fight, or don't report the news they are handed. Whether in the form of a revolt or a turning of the tide, every action that withdraws support from the elite and places that support elsewhere shifts the balance of power and begins to open new possibilities for society.

The elite clearly act in their own interest, largely free from manipulation by others. They gain in subjective well-being, but also, demonstrably, in objective measures like wealth and power. It is interesting to examine the range of motives and rewards in the spectrum of subcultures that make up the balance of society: Some individuals aspire to become elites. Others may falsely imagine themselves to be such. Some find it an honor and thrill to ride on the coattails of the most important people in an important country. Others are content with the trickle-down wealth which has (or had) come with being part of an empire. For many, it is safe and rational to adopt the world view that is offered to them by a powerful government. It is also a rational choice to decide that if you can't beat them, then it is better to surrender and join them. Some people are acting under the spell of elite propaganda and don't know that the messages are deceiving. Some people have a price for their agreeing to follow orders or do ethically questionable things. Sometimes that price is as low as just a steady job and a regular paycheck. Many people are conscientious and strive to make a difference where they see the need. Some apply their sizable talents and make a large impact. Others are discouraged to the point of withdrawing from participation in societal issues.

Taken together, there appear to be a considerable number of people who are acting for relatively narrow self-interests. There seems to be no shortage of individuals willing to take a role in human endeavors associated with damage to the natural world or to the health and well-being of other people, directly or indirectly. That there are people willing to level vast swaths of the world's rainforests, blow up pristine Appalachian mountaintops, aggressively market sugary beverages linked to an established health epidemic, deafen whales with sonar and underwater explosives, or create fraudulent scientific studies is a discouraging sign. In the decades since the end of the Vietnam War there has been, on balance, an attitude of indifference to US covert intervention overseas, as well as to the rightness or wrongness of our outright wars. Beyond Occupy Wall Street and the turnout against invading Iraq in 2003, there is not a strong recent precedent for US citizens challenging the status quo in large numbers. (The Seattle protests of 1999 might have been a sign of a burgeoning new activism that was merely driven underground by the crackdown on protests that followed.) In their own way, shape, and form, many US citizens are allowing rule by the few, for the few.

Ironically, there could be less reason to be discouraged by some of the behavior choices of highly placed individuals in business and government than by the choices of lower-level employees whose collaborative roles cannot merely be explained by their compensation. We could hope that a conscience would override a smaller salary, where it might not as easily a larger one.

A partial explanation for the degree to which people seem to support, or "vote for," elite interests is found in the persuasion and manipulation that remain a steady part of the US media landscape. We have pointed out that there is a battle on for our minds. The many ways individuals can gain by influencing the behavior of others fuels an onslaught of attempts to do just that. The biologists' notion of manipulation by parasites is a close parallel, wherein the ability to act on behalf of our own well-being can be hijacked, so that others gain through controlling our actions. In his book *Fifteen Steps to Corporate Feudalism—How the Middle Class Eliminated Itself,* Dennis Marker illustrates the degree to which we have been hoodwinked into acting against what would appear to be in our best interest. He documents how a percentage of the US population has handed its wealth and power to the elites by acquiescing to a broad range of changes beginning, in his narrative, with the Reagan administration. The most obvious "correction" that could be made in US society is to close the gap between what people think is in their interest, and what really is in their interest by objective measures: to, in other words, somehow counteract or negate elite-generated persuasion and manipulation.

The larger part of this fight for independence of our thoughts is psychological. Access or exposure to reliable facts is, on its own, not enough. Grappling with truths and fictions in the political sphere may encounter some of the same complex terrain that applies to personal growth and to mental well-being in general. Governments can certainly symbolize parents, and needs for security and cognitive harmony run deep. Could a counseling or psychotherapy approach be applied to expanding people's awareness of their place in society and to gaining a better understanding of our natural needs for conformity, affirmation, or safety? To be accommodated to a dysfunctional society or family can mean there is no motivation to change. It may be true that we need to become unhappy or unsettled on the way to engaging a desire to fully right our circumstances.

Activist efforts may do better focusing on educating, recruiting, persuading, and also censuring the enablers of the elite, rather than protesting to the elite directly. In the "information war," material can be channeled to these "guards," including soldiers (for whom the stakes are the highest) to catalyze a change of heart about their cooperation in antidemocratic practices. It is a hugely discouraging reality that the US seems to be able to find rank-and-file collaborators in virtually every country it engages—individuals willing to take part in sometimes heavy-handed repression of their own people. Conceivably, they too could be addressed through educational or subversive materials. Crafting the right message for the "guards" may be a strategic best focus: that tier holding the most potential for undercutting elite control.

Mustering power

When corruption has overtaken a democracy, and a government is being run by and for a minority elite, the public has a very specific task for itself. Since power is the decisive factor that that public is now short on, their challenge involves finding power where it resides, assembling that power into a larger force, directing it where it needs to go, and ultimately growing the power they have—all toward the goal of matching or exceeding the consolidated power of the elite. This is the essential process that can turn the tide back to the balance that a fair society depends on.

In talking about the forces that vie for influence in a society and a country, we did not try to talk about numbers. But numbers make a few simple points clear. A 1 percent of the population represents a relatively small number of people such that, even with greatly consolidated wealth, the other 99 percent could probably easily flex a mightier amount of power. And it may be true that 70 percent, 50 percent, or an even smaller percentage of the public has as much power as a top 1 percent. Thus, an elite could be readily countered if blocks of power on this scale were to be harnessed. This leads us, finally, to the real-life picture of groups in society that pool, aggregate, or compile their power in order to have the influence that they do. In effect, the concentrated power of the few can be answered by combining the disbursed power of the many. Emblematic of this is the formation of alliances and collaborations that achieve things the same individuals or groups could not achieve independently. This time-honored means by which power imbalance in societies has been rectified is embodied in the graphic image of a school of small fish turning on a pursuer and assembling themselves into an even larger fish.

Working strategically with power that already exists in society is one way to achieve a social change goal. The second general approach to countering concentrated power is to take the power that one has and grow it. This is also an iconic process. We have observed that if power can be used to gain more power, how can someone without much power possibly hope to catch up? Individuals in society who overcome a socioeconomic disadvantage to rise from "rags to riches" give us one clear example of how this is done. The formula involves hard work, discipline, cultivating connections, gaining knowledge or education, keeping an eye out for opportunities, and sacrificing in the present for the longer term. The principle of using a little in order to gain more and using more to gain still further scales up perfectly to apply to society-wide social movements. These two modalities—working smartly with the power one has and growing power—operate hand-in-glove in the real world: aligned interest groups change the playing field, which shifts power as an outcome, catalyzing more initiatives, and more and different alliances in the process.

We have been describing power as a quantitative measure of the ability we each have to influence our broader environment—to influence, in other words, the world around us. In addition, we have referred to it as a wild card for the reason that power can have many expressions and take many forms. We can picture a powerful person as someone with the financial leverage to rattle the economy. But we can also picture an individual who captures the imagination of the world by an inspired act. Our power depends, in part, on what we are made of inside, on what we believe, and what we value. This is the source from which our motivations flow, and strong motivation is a component of strong power. Knowledge and information are central to our power. Our ability to comprehend, analyze, communicate, or strategize all depend on this knowledge and information, as well as on raw intelligence, and integrative functions like wisdom and judgement. Power lurks in ideas that awaken, inform, or inspire other people. The more certainty we have in our studied conclusions, the more readily and confidently we can act when opportunities arise. Expressions of power emerge from deep sources within our makeup. Gumption has power, as do conviction and audacity.

Having power, and utilizing it, however, are two separate things. Just as a cartoon miser may count their gold all day instead of putting it to use, the average person has capacity that may be unused, underused, or even undiscovered. Power is a capability that can go on to be fulfilled or expressed.

A person who is a celebrity may, at times, have a lot of power. They always have the ear of the press, for instance. But they are not powerful if they do not have control of their reputation. Many a prominent person has been turned into a kook or philanderer by the media in the time it takes to dot the "i" in incapacitate! If someone is bribable, then they have less power as a result. To have no fear is powerful in a way. Fearlessness has its place. But if a fearless act leads to damage to one's life and limb, or leads to being locked away, then agency may come to an end. Martyrdom can play a role even then, but in rare circumstances.

Life delivers opportunities to each of us for exerting greater influence. There are times when we are in the spotlight, when all eyes are on us to see what we will do or say, when we have leverage or the deciding vote, when we can step forward as an authority or an expert. Key moments with this chance to act and make a difference may be fleeting.

A person may shy away from controversy in order to protect their reputation. But shouldn't reputations be founded on, and reflect, the most important parts of who we are? Wouldn't we want people to know what we believe? If you "lose" your reputation doing things you believe in, then it just means you needed to find new friends or colleagues who would praise and support you in your choices. Yet it is also true that by concealing one's beliefs, a person can use a "reputation" strategically for aiding their advancement or achievement, and for acquiring or holding onto power. This approach may be part of an individual's strategy for social change.

It can easily be argued that the American Revolution would not have been won when and how it was, without the galvanizing and inspirational words of Thomas Paine—including those lines penned at the most dispirited moments in the campaign. Words can change the course of history. Every bit of time and care devoted to refining the form and content of the messages we fashion increases the impact they have in the milieu of the culture. Taking language to the level of art is instinctual for humans and heightens the drama of political discourse, as we witness sometimes fierce public competition among ideas. Entering into this fray tests the mettle of citizens and of social change advocates and begins to reveal which views are capable of winning hearts and minds, and which are not.

Included in the potential artfulness of our communicating can be any of the elements of good theater, which are what they are because of their very ability to move us and stir our emotions. If being artistic equates with something being a compelling form of communication, then we could say that art, in its many mediums, deserves to be at the center of social change activity. Humans have been designed by nature so that emotions arise in us to guide our actions. Emotions are our way of registering both where we stand in life and what the prospect of our different choices each "feel" like. Rationality may seem like an alternative to emotion, but any thought or idea with implications for our fate will naturally trigger specific and informative emotions. Our power, therefore, may be at its most effective when we influence the way that people feel. Successfully stirring the emotions of others is the larger part of actually leading them to act differently.

While it may take some looking to find the right platforms for our own outspokenness, a choice we almost always have is to support or defend an outspoken person whom we believe in. As a general orientation, we can throw whatever weight we have behind each positive development we spot. At minimum, this weight can cumulatively take the form of public opinion, which is a part of the shaping of cultural trajectories. One path for the expression of personal power falls to the simple notion of bravery and of courage. How many of us know perfectly well what things we *could* do—things that we have the right skills and knowledge to do, and that we know would be helpful or productive?

When individuals with the same interests band together, their resulting power is at least additive and potentially synergistic (meaning the result is greater than the sum of the parts). The very act of networking discrete groups together can lead to growth-type phenomena—not unlike a nervous system with its rudimentary components but extraordinary capabilities.

The full potential of an individual or a group is often not easy to judge because of the phenomenon of a limiting factor. If so-and-so had access to higher education, they might become a famous scientist; if another person only had land to work, they could easily support their family through farming; if this other person had access to a line of credit, they would flourish as an entrepreneur. The non-elites of the world live with more limiting factors than elites do. The revelation hidden in this fact is that a majority of humanity has vast untapped potential that is currently being unexpressed because of different versions of a lack of power. What this implies is that, as power increases among the public, it will tend to generate activity that naturally grows more power for those individuals. People usually both know how and are eager to solve their problems and advance their welfare. To give them added power would be to open floodgates of constructive activity.

When it comes to measuring power, there must surely be a difference between power that can be sustained, and power that is susceptible to being lost. This presents an interesting way to evaluate the power of both the elite and the wider public. If power is dependent on maintaining a fiction, for instance, then this is a weak position that is vulnerable to exposure. It is power with a precariousness. Power that is built on an unassailable truth cannot be shaken off its pedestal. For this kind of reason the appearance of someone being very powerful may be less true than at first glance. At minimum, this view can be cast as an opportunity to look for chances to undercut an opponent's position by exposing a fallacy or deceit. Leveling the playing field includes making it less tenable to lie, and makes that a riskier choice.

Available time, energy, and finances are finite for each of us and put limits on our exercise of power. In countless places and situations in the world, the maw of human need is so great that if a person commits to sharing what they have in order to help others, it becomes a practice with no end. There is a terrible irony here in that elites have given compassionate people lifetimes worth of things to try to address—and, by some reasoning, these people have to choose between helping those causes and individuals directly or countering what may be the same problems at their source.

Finally, there are also those who, individually, already have a great deal of power. Wealthy and influential people with a vision for a just society have the capacity to be major actors in social transformations. Pursuing alliances with such individuals, including simpatico elites, makes sense. In general, elites will be the ones who have the most potential to influence other elites and can pursue their own alliances in the course of this.

Motivation

For individuals to mount an effective challenge to elite-cornered wealth and power, there needs to be impetus. The capability we each have for shaping the world around us cannot be separated from our motivation to do so. The more motivated we are, the harder we will work toward any goal. Sources of motivation for political engagement and for social change are abundant, and can be found in all the familiar places.

In life, people wish for good health, bodily comfort, the chance to seek fulfillment of many kinds, economic security, and happiness itself—all things that we would go to some effort to secure. If any of these are under threat, we have reason to sit up and pay attention.

Leaving the world a better place for our children is a big idea, and one that unites all cultures. Equally big, the progression of civilization is so grand a story that its perpetuation in a noble form is something which will always inspire people in how they lead their lives.

Added motivation for defending rights and freedoms can be found in realizing that we inherited them from others who sacrificed in order to gain them. We could think in terms of owing a debt of gratitude to these forebears, or of not allowing their efforts to have been in vain.

Humans are oriented to identify with—and act in—groups. Camaraderie—sometimes fueled by righteousness—is one of our strongest emotions and motivators. It is the glue that holds a sports team together, and it will lead people to, for instance, enlist to fight in wars. In our own countries and in the wider world, we will readily bond with, or work on behalf of, people with whom we have a shared vision.

The reality of nuclear weapons, we can assume, provides all the motivation needed for us to leave no stone unturned in working for abiding world peace.

It is motivating to feel that we are part of a vanguard, or that we are participating in charting an untrodden path. New perspectives and paradigms may be something people hunger for and will be inspired to support. People can be discouraged to work for nominal reforms, but ready to get excited about ambitious new ideas, with the possibilities they present.

We are motivated to do things that we expect to be fun. The more fun a revolution is, the better the turnout will be.

Savvy and wise

If arousing motivation to improve society is half of what it takes to meet with success, then being smart as we go about it is the other half. Societies are complex like ecosystems are complex, and understanding human society well enough to steer its course is a tall order. Albert Einstein has been paraphrased as saying that, when undertaking an investigation, one should try to make things as simple as possible, but no simpler. This mantra serves every kind of scientist well, and is the line one walks in order to home in on what is true. Starting with a sense of what is true and accurate for society, more and more integrated approaches will be needed to help solve multiple interrelated issues as efficiently as possible. This includes looking for root causes of problems, as well as for pivotal or key points for intervention—again, with the notion that addressing one thing can have cascading effects up and down the line. Tools like flow diagrams that map society's interactions, or computer simulations that take us to hypothetical futures in the blink of an eye help distill useful knowledge out of this complexity. Because of the nature of non-linear systems, we should be ready to search in unexpected places for ideas on how to initiate change. The more savvy, knowledge, skill, and wisdom that exists within the public, the more effectively we will be able to address present and future challenges.

There is a dominant and explicit message in the US that we are beyond needing to be introspective or self-critical as a nation. We are supposed to be the model country which other countries can measure themselves against. This exemption, however, is unsound. Introspection and self-scrutiny are as valuable for a citizen to their country as they are in our personal lives—both with the potential to open up new ways of seeing and acting. Regarding the projected image of the US, it must be remembered that a powerful nation's stories will always paint it in a good light—both in the present and in history books. Again, this is not to be cynical—it is just what would be predicted.

Since alliances are central to countering elite power, savvy among the public needs to include an appreciation that others may intentionally try to create divisiveness in order to prevent people from joining forces. Sidestepping such provocations, attitudes that welcome allying and collaborating generate more chances to augment power.

Until the playing field is leveled, doing the right thing for broader society and for the natural world will be more expensive than the alternatives. Weaning ourselves off the notion that we should be entitled to the lowest price when buying, the highest price when selling, and the highest return when investing can help put our minds at ease as we make our economic choices, and allow us to better enjoy the positive feeling of a harmonious conscience. If this remedial reality is assumed and fully appreciated, then it is easier for people to act in accord with it.

There are quite a number of things—animate and inanimate, current and future—that are not able to advocate for themselves in the arena of society today. Future generations for one, certainly have a stake or interest in decisions that we are making without their actual input. Nature, similarly, does not get to vote, so we have to serve as its proxy if we want its "voice" to be heard. People have a choice to act on behalf of others, including inhabitants of foreign lands. Anyone who has little power and is suffering is in need of other individuals who can advocate for them. This is a very human and important activity: choosing to aid and defend each other when it is needed.

A case can be made that we do not qualify for, or have not earned, the chance to take many more risks on Earth today because we have essentially used up the ecological buffer that would enable us to do so, and be fine in the end. All ecological systems are currently in decline by a range of measures, not the least of which is the remaining number of different species they contain. From an empirical point of view, we lessen the ability to track and understand things such as environmental illnesses every time we introduce a new variable like an untested industrial chemical. The wisdom that comes from learning and heeding good science could and would serve humanity well. One principle that is underappreciated is that the point of reference for ideal human health is the environment of our evolutionary past. By definition, the best match between our genes and their environment was just prior to the era in history when culture began to change faster than genes could keep up. Every novel addition to our environment since then has been a gamble and an experiment of sorts. Some developments have enhanced our welfare, some have not. Of these changes, the hardest to evaluate will be those which interact with life on a molecular scale, such as nanotechnology, synthetic chemistry, 5G-type technologies, or increased levels of ionizing radiation. The rule of thumb is that any unprecedented kind of interaction with our biochemistry is likely to be for the worse—given the extraordinary fine-tuning of our body systems.

The well-known precautionary principle (akin to better safe than sorry) embodies what would be a wise and ethical decision-making philosophy for humans. Along similar lines, the Iroquois entreaty to consider the next seven generations includes the advice to think through consequences as far as is possible and reminds us that care and concern for our descendants is a good thing, not to be neglected or discounted in the course of being absorbed in the present. What we don't want to have happen is for the fallout from declining abundance or prosperity in the world to lead to less caution, less prudence, or to a focus on short-term gain—to, in other words, survival mode. The advocates for acting on behalf of the future would normally at least be parents, grandparents, uncles, and aunts. A hypothetical generation that had no children could have an incentive to "not waste perfectly useful things" and use up everything itself. Let us therefore hope, or ensure, that the science fiction writers' portrait of pollution-caused infertility in society does not come true, and result in a downward spiral of narrowing interests, leading to further pollution, leading to narrowing interests.

A smart choice that could easily be lost in the shuffle of discussion over other issues is to avoid, at all cost, things that damage germline DNA (as opposed to somatic cell DNA). A chilling prospect for humanity is an unstoppable perpetuation of genetic damage, with its manifestation in ill health and other hampering abnormalities. The same misfortune could befall the animal and plant world, as well, through no fault of its own. But in their case, selective survival has the capacity to re-refine an organism's genome, particularly where generation times are short.

It can be tragic if, in hindsight, we wish we had had better foresight. What would we feel, for example, about our choices and priorities today if we could look back from thirty, fifty, or a hundred years in the future? Even with the best guesses of experts, it is not easy to conjure up a future world, but there may be things to learn about ourselves and what we most value if we attempt the exercise.

There are many situations in life where a sacrifice leads to a later reward. We should expect a large number of opportunities to sacrifice in the years ahead, in order to usher positive changes into position. Decades of shortcuts in society are part of what explains the need for this phase. But there is nothing that says a sacrifice needs to feel like a sacrifice!

Efforts to equalize wealth and power should avoid scenarios in which it is redistributed downward from the middle- or upper-middle-income tiers, leaving the most consequential, stratospheric power untouched. True, that power may be the hardest to reach, but it cannot safely be left as is. If we take power from those with an intermediate amount, then this might weaken a potential ally.

Though we have been emphasizing a quest for a relative equality of political power, what really is most important is that a stable or equilibrium point is reached, where the gap between those with more and with less ceases to widen. Stability, after all, means there *isn't* positive feedback. It is safe to guess that the current imbalance of power in the US is not a spread that can be stable in this way as there is simply too much "muscle" on one side. It is interesting to wonder just how much rebalancing would be needed to make an equilibrium a realistic possibility: perhaps a distribution such as existed in the 1960s or 1970s, and with the civic engagement to maintain it.

Vigilance/participation

The path we are on in the US (and much of the Western world by extension) may best be seen as a default path. It is the product of those individuals who have most actively sought to shape it and is the result of the absence of full participation by others. There may, in other words, be a partial vacuum of activity—one that can be filled by citizens who would choose to be proactive in their own right in creating the world they wish for. In some countries, in some battles, people use, and fight with, every bit of power they have. In the US and the West it appears that we have the chance to use unused power and to see what that can achieve.

If at any time the public does not think the government is doing a good job at its "assignments," there is a great deal that can be done to make up the difference, so to speak. Things that citizens can do themselves include: making peace with other peoples around the world; measuring or monitoring pollutants; tracking shady financial networks; recording violations of human rights; or directly providing assistance to people in need—not to mention writing about, or documenting, what one does. All of these activities contribute to rebalancing power—and without having to win a single election! Thousands of organizations outside of governments are daily engaged in just such accountability and service work in the world, some of which could be likened to a global "neighborhood watch" program—keep-

ing an eye on things that need keeping an eye on. Third-party cer-
tification projects are similar to this and have become quite common
for things such as trade or labor practices, the treatment of animals,
or the ingredients in our food. In all likelihood, this kind of documentation will be extended to provide better accounting in yet more
arenas.

Many people would agree that the multi-century rampage
through the resources of North America—from pelts to lumber to
whales to fisheries to coal to oil to fresh water to minerals to natural
gas—has left us poorer instead of richer. A bonafide need to question
the notion of "extracting wealth" most certainly now applies to the
resources of the world. One hundred years ago John Muir lamented
that "nothing dollarable is safe," as he watched exploiters move in
on the natural treasures of Yosemite Valley. Still, today, the public
does not have the leverage needed to be adequate protectors of commons resources and of nature in general. Where activist work con-
sistently fails or meets a roadblock, it may be a sign that the "up-
stream" problem is power imbalance.

Whether or not a country is susceptible to factions corrupting it
from within is only half of the story of what watchful citizens must
consider. Vigilance against external takeover is also part of the picture of protecting domestic power and sovereignty. As we touched
on in Chapter Three, takeover or infiltration by a foreign entity runs
the spectrum from overt and military to many versions of covert and
stealthy, including through the use of propaganda. Whether one lives
in El Salvador, the Ukraine, or in the US itself, people with foreign
allegiances taking up positions of influence and power within your
country is an example of the kind of thing to look out for. Laws often
do exist for this protective purpose, but these can be outwitted, just
as rules to prevent endogenous subversion can. If there were outsiders infiltrating the US, it can be guessed that at least some domestic elites would be in alliance with them, since elites, in general, are

less apt to be fooled into acting against their interests than is the average citizen.

World patterns

At this point in history, the question of which societies are vulnerable to spawning their own ruinous elite is less important than what to do with instances of the power accumulation cycle being already underway, advanced, and expressing itself internationally. Currently, there are virtually no countries left on the planet that have not been subjected to attempts at control by the Western power block—such is the stage of this dynamic. The puzzle of how to reclaim or to implement fair and democratic governance across all countries affected by this pattern is multilayered and increasingly deserves to be approached and addressed on a planet-wide scale.

One way to look at the layout of the globe presently is that the centers of Western power have created subordinate clones, or self-similar "offspring," throughout the world. This group can be roughly identified by the presence of US military bases on their soil—currently numbering eighty countries (according to David Vine, author of *Base Nation: How US Military Bases Abroad Harm America and the World*). The co-option process behind this has replicated and disseminated a non-democratic, or weakly democratic, model in these countries, and almost everywhere this template exists, populations are working at trying to gain or regain power. We could expect that the subversion these countries have undergone is the product of an internal, aspiring elite, supported by and collaborating with a stronger external elite, to the mutual benefit of each. It remains an interesting and important question whether many or any of these countries could have been corrupted to the extent that they have without the substantial sponsorship of a major power. It is worth wondering, in other words, whether or not fair societies could be the norm—but for the rare, too powerful, group that willfully overrides moral considerations and notions of fair play, as they pursue their objectives.

Though there is obvious asymmetry in this global layout, there is also an interdependence that has important ramifications. A subordinate country's elites only have the power that they do because of support from the dominating country. So if the dominating country elites were to lose against a domestic rebellious public (picture the US in this case), then subordinate countries would also likely fall to their rebellious publics. The interdependence comes in that the dominating country gains significant wealth, resources, and strategic positioning from subordinate countries. If enough of the subordinate countries were to successfully reject foreign control, then the dominating country would be weakened in turn, possibly with cascading consequences that undercut its power further.

There are many ways in which interests line up for peoples around the world. Social movements in various countries are often working toward the same objectives, only from different vantage points. Learning what it takes to interface with individuals in other countries is a step toward creating global networking, and to finding or affirming common ground. Creativity is called for in developing global alliances that counter undemocratic forces. The more bridges that can be built between groups with shared interests, the more effective they can jointly be.

It is important to distinguish who has what capacity to effect change in a corrupted country. Some people have virtually no power to influence either their own governments or the countries that may control their governments. The same way that a hostage is usually powerless to secure their own rescue, some countries and populations may depend on outside interventions to free them. More commonly, people may work with different capabilities and constraints from both inside and outside of corrupted countries simultaneously. "Rescuing" the world from aggressor nations may fall to a specific collection of individuals and countries that have the right combination of insight, leverage, finesse, or raw might to make the key moves to achieve this.

A search for ethical rules of how to respond to an opponent could settle on the idea that no physical force should be used in defense if no physical force is used in offense, with the corollary that physical force is justified as defense against physical force. So while we have primarily talked about nonviolent strategies for rebalancing power, there is also a vast topic of the strategic use of weapons and force to win against aggressors. If a powerful entity is committed to using violence to enlarge its power, then the strategic questions for how to respond are particularly challenging. Once upon a time there were choices like building a Great Wall of China or castles with moats—emphasizing defense. Fleeing from an aggressor's advances is one choice, which usually means forfeiting assets and even one's country. This is the lifesaving instinct that accounts for many of the world's refugees today.

The asymmetrical relationship between a populace and an elite has been the main focus in these chapters. But there are, of course, also contests in the world between more closely matched groups, and even very closely matched groups or nations. Where the growing power of the Western/NATO alliance could, in theory, be stopped by their own populations or by the peoples of the countries they invade or exploit, it is now clear that this alliance could also be stopped by countries like Russia and China.

The grandest design of Western elites appears to be to create what is referred to as a unipolar world, in which their alliance subsumes the whole globe and becomes the sole superpower. An alternative future vision—that of a multipolar world—is one in which individual national sovereignty remains, multiple large powers coexist, and interactions between nations follow rules and guidelines that have been mutually decided. Versions of the unipolar or united world (contrasted to multipolar) could, as well, be entered into by choice, without coercion, and be like a federation of nations, in one model.

If strong national autonomy is not part of the elite's image for a future unipolar world, then it should not surprise us if national power is already on the wane. Nations, in fact, could cease to be the salient unit of organization in such a world order. Increasing supranational control, as exemplified by a lineage of proposed trade deals, could leave citizens of the US in a situation not unlike a country of the Global South, with a figurehead leader, and suffering under an austerity regimen. We may be slowly joining the ranks of people who no longer have sway over their governments and who do not have the power, or even a mechanism, to find and influence the true centers of control. Has, indeed, our story in the US come full circle with us again becoming a "colony" to a larger power? This matter-of-fact assessment reinforces the simple idea that it is easy to solve some problems early on, harder after they are more advanced, and impossible beyond a point, as when avenues for change have all but disappeared.

Wrap-up

Referring to society as a self-organizing system is not meant to be an esoteric way of characterizing or understanding it. It is meant to be the most basic, accessible, and accurate way to picture the phenomenon of culture and how it comes to be. Humans, with their naturally selected behavior apparatus, are willful and have agency. We *drive* the system. But by stepping back far enough, the hope is to see society as more than just a human perpetual-motion machine. The hope here is to see patterns that emerge through time that tell us important things we would want to know about how society works and what we can do to improve it. We have taken society apart into many pieces—into snippets that at least enable us to wrap our minds around individual building blocks of culture and glimpse how outcomes are shaped or determined. We have looked at what I refer to as the logic of social systems—at what could be thought of as the mathematical reasoning at work just below the surface in this particular system called society. This logic includes patterns that can stabilize things, magnify things, or sort by different criteria. It includes the extensive chains of cause and effect that interlace society, and the details of contests between individuals, businesses, and nations.

For one perspective on the nature of what exists, recall that everything we see around us on Earth, and beyond, is there because it had something going for it that the things that are not around did not. For the things that *are* around, there are reasons and explanations for them being the way they are. For the things that are *not* around, there are, accordingly, reasons why they are not. There is a story behind all outcomes, whether we are talking about a molecule, a life form, a hair style, or the particular persons on a board of directors. Puzzling out these stories in any realm helps demystify the world around us and elevates our experience of being alive on this remarkable planet. Puzzling out the stories behind outcomes in culture is a subset of this, and the knowledge it engenders turns out to be an important element in the power we ultimately have to shape our world. The explanations for all of our human triumphs and travails (as well as commonplace experiences) are there to be found when we go looking for them.

Recall, also, that in culture things do not necessarily win or survive because they are good or fair or are the will of the people. They survive because of the logic of surviving. It is therefore prudent for us to be questioning the worth, as well as the how and why, of what it is that prevails, so that we can do better than to be at the mercy of some of the dominant processes determining these outcomes. In the broadest picture, the constituents that make up culture can be explained as an ongoing winnowing of an also ongoing creation of the new. In this process, everything in human culture is perpetually being adjusted to comport with the preferences of individuals and the groups and alliances they form. One type of determinant for what survives is whether or not something has defenders or advocates. Things that are fought for, or advocated for, are more likely to survive. This goes for governing structures, public services, historic districts, natural wonders, as well as rights and freedoms.

If US foreign and domestic policy both look as if they were the fulfilled wish list of the country's largest corporations or wealthiest citizens, just notice that that is what has won, and think back to our many reasons why it could be so. The person who wins the contract, the candidacy, the bailout, the subsidy, the lawsuit, the exemption, the battle, the honors—that person may win what they do because of the power they have in society's contests. Explanations for what prevails are sometimes as involved and protracted as the elimination tournament of the US Major League Baseball championship. Or the details of a contest can be as short as the few key moves that decide a game of tic-tac-toe.

This grouping of individuals we have been referring to as the "elite" is nothing more than the cluster of people who have had the most success at gaining and holding onto power. This is often achieved through character traits like intelligence and drive. But in the most stripped-down model, this kind of success can come about via one simple pattern—namely, that gained power enhances the ability to gain power. Assuming humans who desire power in the first place, the natural outcome of this dynamic is that any divergence in the distribution of power in society will begin to magnify itself, leading to a subculture that can be designated as an elite. This, fortunately, is only the simplest setup. More realistic and involved systems can lead to other outcomes. Yet the threat of this particular scenario pushing itself through even the fabric of a complex and long-established society remains, so fundamental is its logic. The suggestion we started with in Chapter One—that the main problems of civilization trace to this particular feature of society as a system—could be reassuring in that the dynamic it describes is so straightforward. It is understandable when people shy away from things that are complicated, and that defy our attempt to fully grasp them. The simplicity of the idea that equality can gravitate to inequality through feedback logic could mean that the concept is, by contrast, easy to evaluate, engage, or wrestle with as an idea relevant to our collective well-being. We can conclude that it does not require unusual circumstances for an elite to emerge in a society. It is also important to notice that an outcome as extreme as tyranny can come about relatively innocently. Since society is built by the actions of individual humans, the one simple choice to always take the path of the most material gain can lead inexorably to something this untoward.

When a society is highly competitive, a person's best choice for themselves is often to also be competitive. Or if society is lawless, others will smartly sense that those are the rules of engagement at that moment in history and join the fray. Yet, the very same people may be happy to take part in a lawful or ethically-guided arrangement if they can trust that it will be reliably that way. There should and could, in fact, be great relief in not having to be perpetually on guard in an aggressive or uncertain environment. The kind of mutability that would allow very different states like this for our human groupings is mirrored in a series of remarkable observations of baboon social dynamics in the wild. In their work studying stress in baboon hierarchies, scientists Robert Sapolsky and Lisa Share came across an example of a baboon troop where, with the sudden absence of the troop's most aggressive alpha males, the remaining baboons became cooperative and less competitive. Further, Sapolsky and Share found that the new social tone was conveyed to immigrating baboons, as well as to future generations within the troop. In human society, if the alpha males/females were somehow not allowed to set the standard when and where they do, this might have a similar result. This is about the "environment" we refer to that can bring forth any number of responses from our multifarious human personalities. It could make sense that there are sets of behaviors that work together as a package, just the way a family would have roles that people choose based on the roles of others. These "sets" may behave like attractors, and factors of one sort or another could disrupt an existing pattern and allow a new one to coalesce, as was the case in this particular baboon troop.

Humanity is in a high-stakes game against the logic of a number of things. Some of these have to do with the essential viability of us as living organisms. But the bulk of them come down to the subjective experience of what our dignity requires, or what our esthetics yearn for. There is a spectrum of potential qualities of life that, for better or for worse, have no real reference point against which they can or should be measured. A benchmark for biological splendor and natural beauty that a human living in North America five hundred years ago had, can barely be compared to the modern experience of nature in the twenty-first century. Our world can become pauperized without us even being aware of what we no longer have or can no longer experience. This is true, too, for such things as liberty or privacy. The idea referred to as "shifting baselines" tells us that many things of value are only judged relative to what we have known in our lifetime. Each generation that is born with less does not know what they are missing, that previous generations had once known. Incrementally, expectations are lowered, allowing a standard to drop and drop further. How far can this process go? And if such an erosion does not stop, then what is left of the human experience beyond some undefined point? Are humans destined to live with chronic ill-health, chronic hard-to-name yearnings, chronic frustrations, less happiness? This is not for any one of us to answer, since well-being is a personal thing. But, as an aid to making wise choices, such questions are worth asking.

When species are gone, there will be no comfort in pointing to who was most responsible for the loss if we even attempt to figure that out. Destroyed architectural treasures, lost lives, erased ecosystems, missing primeval forests when lost are lost for good. This "gone forever" is the measure of how important our choices are today. Here there is no taking the exam over again till we pass it, getting back in shape after a sedentary winter, or making a smarter purchase next time. Many things that give life meaning may be at stake, each with a closing window in which to act. If the concept of rule-by-the-many fails, then the world will be run, instead, by a minority elite. Besides the many important social implications of this path for civilization, the elite have not demonstrated an ability to be good stewards of the earth, and so may quickly seal its fate as unable to support life as we know it.

Scattered throughout these pages are most of the components of a model for analyzing society, including definitions and some vocabulary. I have not, however, tried to walk through our various examples using this template to describe steps in a process. It can be done for each turn of the discussion, but I don't believe it was necessary in order to make the points we have made. The model is there as a suggested tool to use when and if it is needed to deepen an exploration of the goings-on within this social system in which we live.

For some, there may be a sense that intransigent problems are just the way of the world—that factors within those problems will defy their being easily solved. When a problem persists, however, it is a clue that the people for whom it is a problem do not have enough power—since, if they did, they would solve it. This is truer than we are often led to believe and helps us to refocus the very notion of how to approach problems. Focusing on the power distribution of the "players" in society may be the true Rosetta Stone that helps us get to the bottom of even our most pressing difficulties. The amount of creative energy and the number of initiatives that would come into force if power does grow among the non-elites is the most hopeful thing on the horizon today. This is the feedback that would flood our world with positive developments if it can be set loose by the passing of the right tipping point and by the removal of obstacles to the projects that humans are so hungry to work on.

The prospects for the future of US democracy—and the consequent ramifications for the world—do depend on the status of elite power and control. But, more importantly, those prospects depend on the qualities and character traits extant in the citizenry as a whole. They depend on the people who would bear the mantle of restoring and sustaining a worthy culture, and who would thereby honor the extraordinary inheritance we have all received in the form of cultural and natural riches. Finding our way from a state of extreme global inequality to the equality of political and economic power that is emblematic of democracy is indeed a puzzle. One moral of the story of modern democracies is simply that it is a bigger job than we thought to ensure that goodness prevails and is sustained; it is a bigger job to maintain popular control and to fend off, or hold off, threats to it.

A theory exists that predicts we will not detect the communications of many advanced civilizations from other solar systems, in spite of the fact that there would be, perhaps, thousands of planets in our galaxy that could support life. The disquieting explanation behind this theory is that most technologically advanced extraterrestrial civilizations would have succumbed to cultural factors that sent them back to their equivalent of the Stone Age or to complete extinction. At least one irony here is that a capability to reach out across the vastness of space to communicate with other lifeforms would roughly coincide with the development of a handful of potentially self-destructive technologies. To whatever extent this prediction were to be true, it is clear enough that we on Earth have entered a decisive stage of advancement in which our own future hangs in a balance.

A strong case has been made by scientists that biological evolution would follow nearly identical logic wherever in the universe life emerged. It is possible that the same would be true of the unfolding logic of cultures, where they existed. The reasoning at work in how a social system takes shape, changes, and evolves could have universal features, not least of which might be an inclination toward inequality of power and influence. What if the puzzles associated with our stage of cultural evolution were following patterns not confined to Earth and its inhabitants? Humans, it could be guessed, may not be alone at all in the challenges we are facing at this momentous time in our history.

As we have pointed out, human problems would have been almost impossible to solve even a hundred years ago when there were still vast riches for ravenous imperial powers to exploit, and next to no real means for accountability on a global scale. And now, suddenly, we appear to be boxed in, facing what we are facing: a need for a tightrope walk to a non-precarious future. Human problems *now* can be solved, and in the nick of time, we could say. Our quandary may amount to more than just how to reclaim a democracy. We may be in the midst of the most trying stage in the evolution of a culture—but which *is* just a stage. Perhaps, as in the teenage years of a maturing human, there is something qualitatively different that is right around the corner.

Appendix

In the preceding chapters I have used an approach to analyzing and understanding human society that I can now summarize here, as follows:

Sensibly enough, nearly everything that transpires in the human arena originates with the actions of humans. To effectively investigate that arena one, therefore, has to understand how we act and how we behave. There are two ways to learn about this: observation and theory. A study of evolutionary biology enables us to make fairly precise predictions about what behaviors would have enhanced our fitness—and thereby been selected—and which would not. This is the theory that gives us insight into human behavior. Alternatively, observing humans in action—including through planned experiments—has cumulatively given us a great depth of understanding into how we act as we do. Together, this becomes the field of psychology.

While it may sound mechanistic, it is accurate to think of humans as individual, autonomous, active agents that collectively create the society we live in. This approach gives us a bottom-up, self-organizing perspective on how society emerges. It is important to notice that if humans tended to behave differently than we do, one would end up with a different consequent society. The behavior of the active agents in a system is key to what transpires.

In a computer lab (or a controlled chemical or ecological experiment) one can launch a system with active agents from scratch and see where it goes. Our human world is already launched, but we can observe where it goes and attempt to understand the how and the why of it. It is correct to think of society as a large system, and we can name all (or most of) the interacting parts that constitute it.

Firstly, in that system, there is the whole of the environment in which we act. This environment includes the physical earth, all of its ecosystems and organisms, all human modifications to the planet, and all of our fellow humans themselves. Each one of us is acting within this environment.

In Chapters One and Four, I made an analogy of humans to computers that I believe is quite apt. Humans have equivalents to a computer's hardware, software, and memory. We have the ability to create output, and we receive inputs through our sensory apparatus. We process inputs and use the equivalent of algorithms to calculate a response. Some of our "hardware" and "software" is determined by genetics, and some of it is shaped by our socialization and learning. Unlike most computers, we can upgrade our own software as we gain knowledge. We would, for instance, typically execute a different algorithm as an adult than we would as a youth in a comparable situation.

When humans are placed in their environment, the following process begins: We each receive information via hearing, seeing, and feeling. We respond in ways that attempt to optimize what we want to optimize. In the course of acting we each shape and change the environment around us. We then respond to this ever-new environment, and on it goes.

There are many ways that social scientists have defined culture. I suggest that a technical definition of culture could be "Every consequence of the use of our muscles to express our will." Muscles are required for virtually every human action, and thus for every contribution an individual makes to the outside world. When culture is defined in this way, then everything about it is concrete and even measurable. The "outputs" of our bodies—whatever we label them as—are there as the tangible things that we see around us and that we respond to every day.

One additional layer to the system humans are embedded within is that our genetic makeup changes through the generations in response to the environment. Since humans shape their environment, they can subsequently shape their own genetic future. While our capacity to make culture was intimately linked to our formative genetics, my feeling is that gene-culture coevolution is a minor factor in the trajectory of human society today. I elected to set this aside as I dealt with the chosen themes in this book.

With large numbers of humans and equally large stretches of time, all of what we know of human history, and up to the present day, is created by us interacting with our broader environment. Fortunately there is some order to what emerges in this process. Looking for and characterizing this order is both the fun and the challenge that a large portion of the world's academic community is engaged in, in one form or another. It is also what I have chipped away at in this book. My strategy in going about this has been to look for patterns and processes in the culture around us, and then to identify the logic that lies behind them.

All of our individual actions, in my model, are to enhance our well-being. Any bad choice is only in retrospect, and "well-being" is broad enough to include altruism, which is its own reward for the given individual. This is a far simpler layout than, for instance, to be labeling our actions as *for* someone else, versus *for* ourselves.

It is interesting to think about how we would "keep score" in the active agent system. What does winning or losing at something result in? Is there anything to quantify? Well-being itself is one candidate, and changes in it do have some influence on our behavior. But it is something that is wholly subjective.

The most useful thing that I found to quantify in the system of society is changes in our ability to influence or impact our environment—a capacity defined here as "power." This turns out to be highly variable among individuals in most modern societies, in part because of feedback loops in acquiring that influence or power. Alliances play a major role in many aspects of human activity, and group size, or the number of one's allies, is another thing that could be quantified in the unfolding system. But alliances can be viewed as the strategic pooling of power, as with getting a half-dozen people together to lift something that could not be lifted alone. Though power is a difficult thing to fully define—and harder still to measure—the reality of it has played a central role throughout the human odyssey.

The notion of quantifying power can be viewed as follows: If we designate the size of a group and specify that power is zero-sum within that group, then the power of each individual can be measured as a percentage of the total. The same kind of measure is frequently used with wealth statistics when, for instance, it may be reported that the wealth of the top 1 percent of individuals is equal to the combined wealth of the bottom 60 percent in a group such as a country or the world. The quantities of wealth or of power are relative to the whole.

With this framework as a starting point, the specifics of the logic at work in the human social system are the primary focus in each of the preceding chapters.

Through examining this logic, we come to understand the origin of the content of society. Lofty as this may sound, I would prefer to bring the whole process down to earth. If we look at a mix of microorganisms on a petri dish, there will be a drama that unfolds. The organisms will each be feeding to maintain their metabolism; they will be bumping up against each other and interacting as they do so; they will be reproducing; they may be attempting to actually destroy a competitor; and they will be gaining or losing territory on the dish as time elapses. How is this different from any number of familiar human dramas that we can name from current events or from the local tabloid? My answer is that much of culture parallels the petri dish drama, while another portion is decidedly different.

Charles Darwin's phrase "descent with modification" is the shortest encapsulation of the theory of natural selection. For organisms, modifications to their DNA are created with each new offspring, and the fittest modifications are selected and subsequently passed on. The evolution of culture has been described using the same template: that culture is passed on from one generation to the next with new modifications that arise on a regular basis.

This process for culture requires a few clarifications.

First of all, with biological evolution, modification is inextricably tied to descent. It is in the formation of gametes and in sexual reproduction that novelty is introduced. Biological descent itself (as in the birth of a new human), has no particular bearing on the content of culture. Descent, for culture, can be pictured, instead, as the learning that maintains continuity through the generations. That learning (descent) goes on throughout each individual's lifetime. Modification, in culture, takes place when humans are creative and inventive. For a given human this may be concentrated in the years when they are at the top of their game in a particular field. So for culture there is a version of descent and a version of modification, both of which differ from their biological counterparts. For culture "descent *and* modification" might be the more accurate phrase.

Culture has continuity through time. But it is not necessarily wholly cumulative. In any era, there may be as many things lost from culture as there are added. Living languages, for example, go extinct every year. And observing the contents of an antiquities museum full of two-, three-, four-, or five-thousand-year-old artifacts is a good place to ask who on Earth today would know how to create such feats of artistry? But continuity is what keeps us from defaulting to a Stone Age life. We reinforce, maintain, and build on the things that interest us, and motivate us, in each generation.

Back to our petri dish example: There is a portion of human culture that does not have much connection to the notion of continuity or to the progression of innovations. There are human counterparts to the dramas that get played out in the lives of virtually every organism—dramas which have been constants for hominid groups since we first walked on two legs. These, of course, involve interactions over resources, mates, food, and territory, and include the spectrum of behavior choices from cooperation to competition. Today if you want to understand the "dramas" related to pollution, poverty, injustice, war, the viability of democracies, or the boom and bust of markets, you will do well looking at psychology and at the logic of games and contests.

Lightning Source UK Ltd.
Milton Keynes UK
UKHW020436160321
380388UK00007B/685